Praise for "Cold Calls to Closing"

"In Cold Calls to Closing, Janet White has laid out the steps, sequence and intricate details of how to be successful at sales, and exposes many of the flaws, missteps and misguided thinking that plague most everyone in sales today. If you're a small business professional, I highly recommend you read this book cover-to-cover and apply the principles; you'll be glad you did."

—**Rich Allen**, Owner, Tour de Profit Business Coaching

"Janet White has written an invaluable book for every business owner. It is optimistic, insightful, sharp-witted and lively, and has all the attributes that have made her so successful. If you're looking for real-world advice about how to win more clients and grow your business, this should be on the top of your reading list."

—**Adam Levy**, Owner, Magnet Sites

"Cold Calls to Closing is a practical guide to sales and marketing for the small business owner that can be put to use immediately. The examples of letters and scripts can easily be modified to give readers a jump start on their own marketing content. Growing a business is as much an internal mind game as external and Janet sums it up perfectly: it's all in your thinking - the result you expect, you get."

—**Joanne Marceau**, Owner, JoAnne Marceau Life Coaching

"Cold Calls to Closing is a handbook for the small businessperson on how to get to the closing on a sale and includes all of the elements it takes to get there. Filled with first-person stories to make the author's points, the book is an easy read and should be a solid reference guide for the solopreneur or any company where the few do much with little. I'd keep a place on my bookshelf for this well-organized and plainly written guide to selling."

—**Paul Maynard**, Director, Events & Relationship Management, North Dallas Chamber of Commerce

"I was very impressed with Cold Calls to Closing." The content, presentation, format and conversational tone are really well done, and will hold your attention and interest right to the end, especially the many pearls of selling wisdom. This book is terrific and will be a valuable asset to sales professionals and novices alike."

—**Richard Peritore**, General Manager, Advanced Tree & Shrub Care, Inc.

"Reading Cold Calls to Closing, as an experienced financial planner and entrepreneur, I was amazed at the similarity in many of the concepts of marketing I have learned over my career. If you follow the precepts and methodology in this book, you will be far ahead of the game of marketing yourself."

—**David Rhodes**, Owner, The Rhodes Financial Group

Cold Calls to CLOSING

What Every Small Business
Should Know About Selling

JANET WHITE

Copyright ©2014 by Janet White

All rights reserved. Printed in the United States of America. No part of this publication may be reproduced, stored in a retrieval system or transmitted in any form or by any means, electronic, mechanical, photocopy, recording or otherwise without the written permission of the author.

Published by The JW Speakers Agency
Plano, TX
(972) 517-7503

www.coldcallstoclosing.com
www.jwspeakersagency.com

Book cover design and formatting by BookCoverCafe.com

ISBN: 978-0-692-23-923-0

Table of Contents

Preface — vii

Part 1 Selling Preliminaries — 1
- **Chapter 1** I Hate to Be Sold — 3
- **Chapter 2** Your Attitude is Everything — 8
- **Chapter 3** Marketing Isn't Selling — 17
- **Chapter 4** Getting Ready to Sell — 34

Part 2 Prospecting/Qualifying — 41
- **Chapter 5** Prospecting/Qualifying Basics — 42
- **Chapter 6** Qualifying Mr. Bigg — 53
- **Chapter 7** First Contact: By Phone — 57
- **Chapter 8** First Contact: By Email/Letter — 76
- **Chapter 9** Sales Letters Makeovers — 94
- **Chapter 10** Following Up — 106

Part 3 Meeting Mr. Bigg — 119
- **Chapter 11** Traditional System Sales Meeting — 120
- **Chapter 12** Contrarian System Sales Meeting — 125
- **Chapter 13** Handling Questions and Objections — 139
- **Chapter 14** Closing is Just an Opening — 154

Part 4 Staying In Touch — 159
- **Chapter 15** After the Sale — 160
- **Chapter 16** Thank You Very Much — 164
- **Chapter 17** Follow-Up Letters — 167

Part 5 Addendum	**171**
Sales Secrets You Didn't Learn in Business School	172
Traditional vs. Contrarian Systems of Selling	175
End Notes	177

Preface

This book is written for you–the small business owner who has little or no formal training in sales, may be frustrated in generating business for your business, and would do just about anything except contacting strangers and asking them to do business with you.

If you have had formal sales training, you may find that some of the advice in these pages is very different from what you have learned. That's because professional salespeople approach selling entirely differently from those who are new to it, know very little about it, may be forced into doing it, and are filled with all kinds of negative emotions about it.

And while this book is geared towards those primarily selling services, if you have a retail store, you may find much of what follows useful, especially if you are dealing with a highly targeted clientele.

Regardless of the kind of business you have and whether you're selling business-to-business (B2B) or business-to-consumer (B2C), you want do more than to simply make sales–you want to establish relationships with individual clients and generate a loyal following of clients, customers and referral sources.

This book will teach you the system of selling I have developed over the years as the result of several experiences I had before the age of 21:

- At 16, I interviewed for my high school newspaper Bruce "Cousin Brucie" Morrow, the top disc jockey at WABC-AM in New York, which was the #1 radio station in America at that time. All it took was a simple fan letter which I thought he'd never see or respond to, or at best, I'd get a form letter that said, *"Thanks for listening."* Instead, he personally wrote back inviting me up to the studio.

- At 17, I got into the college of my choice when I didn't have the grades or the SAT scores, a grant or scholarship, connections on the inside or was a special case, and was told in no uncertain terms by the "experts" that it was impossible.

  Instead of listening to the naysayers and standard advice about how to write my essay and behave in the interview, I followed my instincts, which told me to let the school know in no uncertain terms how very much I wanted to be there.

- At 20, I interviewed for my college newspaper world-renown Broadway composer/lyricist Stephen Sondheim in his Manhattan home. I also booked him to come out to my college to speak for free to my fellow theatre majors.

  All it took was a simple fan letter that said how much we students admired him and his work and that I wanted to interview him. He responded exactly the same way Bruce did—he wrote me back and said, *"Yes."*

- A few months later, I got an internship as a reporter at Newsday on Long Island, working in the city room right along with real reporters and writing stories under my own byline. I found out later I was one of 10 college students selected from a nationwide pool of 1,500 applicants.

As these kinds of experiences would continue to happen to me, they solidified my ever-growing conviction how easy it is to sell or simply, get in and get the "yes," as long as I used the right approach combined with the right mindset. I didn't know what I was doing; all I knew was that whatever it was I was doing worked over and over.

The key element in this process was that I challenged conventional wisdom about what I was supposed to do, how I was supposed to behave, what I could realistically expect from taking certain actions and how things were supposed to happen as a result.

As I began to read traditional sales books, I became very confused when I learned that most people think selling is hard, getting in to see the decision maker is a challenge, and I should expect to be disappointed and frustrated most of the time.

Since that had never been my experience, I was even more confused when I learned traditional sales tactics that were contrary to the approaches I had been using intuitively and which I had proven to be virtually infallible.

In this book, you will learn the sales techniques that have continued to work for me for decades. You will be encouraged to adopt new thoughts and take actions that may seem strange, but will intuitively feel right.

And as you stick with it, you will find that the secret to successful selling has everything to do with how you think about yourself, your business and your clients or customers.

Part 1:
SELLING PRELIMINARIES

Chapter One
I HATE TO BE SOLD

As a human being who happens to be a professional salesperson, I am one of the hardest and easiest people to sell to. I hang up on telemarketers who are obviously reading scripts, delete emails from people who haven't bothered to learn anything about me, what I do or are interested in, and throw out snail mail from people who believe that I would buy from someone who relies on junk mail to get business.

I turn away from pushy salespeople, reply to, *"Can I help you?"* with *"No, thanks, I'm just looking,"* and have stopped salespeople in the middle of their presentations to tell them why I wouldn't listen to them anymore and then teach them how to correctly sell to me.

When I walk past a cosmetic counter in a department store and a saleslady tells me she has a new age-defying skin care line, I dare her to guess my age. (I look at least ten years younger than I am). I then tell her that when a woman with really terrific skin like mine walks up to her counter, she shouldn't try to sell her wrinkle cream.

When a telemarketer from a roofing company calls saying they will be in my area and want to inspect my roof, I ask them where my area is, and if they hesitate because they have to look it up or guess wrong, I hang up.

Because I run a booking agency for speakers, I am frequently contacted by people seeking an agent to help get them paid speaking engagements. In order to convince me that I have to take them on, their email pitches range from the short and sweet, like *"Looking for the right fit for representation, sending intro material and will follow-up, thanks"* to going on and on about their accomplishments in an attempt to impress me.

Each of these would-be clients fails to realize – or never bothers to find out – that my agency only represents local business owners who use free speaking as a way to build their business. We don't and won't represent professional speakers or those who want to be. No matter how good they are or what these people have to say, I'm never going to be interested in them.

In every one of these selling situations, these people lost the sale because they saw me as a prospect, not a person. That's too bad, because they don't know the secret to successful selling:

Nobody likes to be sold, but everyone loves to buy.

On the other hand, when a salesperson asks me questions, engages me in a conversation, makes an attempt to put me at ease and guides me towards making a correct decision, I try to reward them by buying something. And if that decision means I'm not going to buy from them, I reward them by referring other people to them who might.

If the cosmetic saleslady had engaged me in a conversation about my skin, I would have bought something, even if I didn't need it. If the roofing telemarketer had bothered to ask me if I had missing shingles or noticed water stains in the ceiling recently, we might have had something to talk about.

When would-be speakers call or email me seeking information, I give them as much advice as I can. If they are experienced speakers, I refer them to booking agents who handle professional speakers, and if they're just getting started, I educate them on the basics and that every paid speaker starts out speaking for free. Most don't like to hear the truth, but they appreciate it.

Busting Selling Myths

If you hate to sell, it's probably because you're worried you'll turn into a pushy, high-pressured, manipulative, annoying bore like the pesky insurance salesman in the movie *Groundhog Day* who keeps chasing Bill Murray into a puddle.

Or it may be because you think selling is demeaning or unprofessional, especially if you're providing a service. Or you're up against the wall and are forced to sell because you're going to be in deep financial trouble if you don't bring in some business very soon.

You may be great at what you do, but if selling isn't a strong suit of yours, don't despair. It's quite possible that you've bought into some fairly common misconceptions about what selling is, how it works and what is required of you. Each of these misconceptions will be dealt with in depth in this book, but here's a brief overview:

Myth: Selling is pitching and hustling.
Truth: Selling is teaching, explaining and persuading.

If you've ever backed off from a fast-talking, slick salesperson trying to sell you something you don't need or want, used gimmicks to get your attention or won't let you get a word in edgewise, you've just had a lesson in how not to make a sale.

Truly effective selling is actually sharing. It's having a conversation with someone about their needs, interests or concerns and seeing if what you have to offer can benefit them. When you use this approach, it will be clear to your potential clients that you care about them rather than lining your own pockets.

Myth: If they tell you they can't afford it, they can't afford it.
Truth: If they want what you have badly enough, they will find the money.

Whether the situation is urgent like a broken pipe, or is one of desire like a new watch, people will buy from those who can help them solve their problem, fill a need or make them feel good. Price is usually not an issue when the need or desire is big enough.

Myth: People shop price.
Truth: People shop value.
> For years, I bought the cheapest toothpaste I could find because I thought they were all the same. Then my dental hygienist told me how the better quality brands could improve my teeth and gums, so for once, I spent twice as much as usual on a tube to see if she was right. Long story short–she was. I now pick my toothpaste from the top of the shelf, rather than the bottom and happily pay twice as much as I did before.

Myth: The customer is always right.
Truth: The customer is often confused.
> It is very common for clients to ask for one thing when they really want something else because they just don't know what to ask for. They look to you as the expert to help them get what they want or need, even if they don't yet know what that is.

Myth: The worst thing a customer can say is "No."
Truth: The worst thing a customer can say is "Maybe."
> In your encounters with potential clients, you will get several legitimate *"no's"* - they're truly not interested, have no need or don't have the money. Legitimate *"no's"* are good things because they enable you to disqualify those people and move on.
>
> But a *"maybe"* is destructive - it means the person you're talking to isn't convinced, isn't ready to buy any time soon or really doesn't want what you're offering and won't admit it. *"Maybe's"* eat up your time and energy and almost always eventually result in a *"no."*

Myth: There's a lot of rejection in selling.
Truth: There are a lot of people who may decline what you're offering.

Rejection does not exist in business because rejection is personal and business is all about transactions, usually involving money. What does exist in business is a negative response that usually comes in the form of a polite, *"No, thank you."*

Myth: People have to be manipulated or pressured into buying something they don't want.
Truth: If people don't want it, don't need it or don't like who is selling it, they won't buy it.

The only reason anyone buys anything is because doing so will help them solve a problem, fill a need or make them feel good. And it's critically important that they like the person who is selling to them because people do business with people they like.

In our society, there is an underlying "us vs. them" mentality when it comes to selling. The assumption is that your potential customer doesn't want what you have, isn't interested in it and wants you to go away as fast as possible.

Nevertheless, as the seller, you have to get them interested in what you're selling and convince them to change their mind – through presentation, pressure or persistence. But you'll find that if you keep pushing when they keep resisting, you'll end up losing.

If you want to make getting your "yes" as easy as possible, always remember that your potential clients are human beings just like you. In general, what you think is what they think, how you feel is how they feel, and how you respond to being sold is exactly how they respond to it.

Chapter Two
YOUR ATTITUDE IS EVERYTHING

If the thought of having to generate business for your business feels daunting, you probably have worrisome thoughts like these:

- How do I find potential clients?
- How do I get past the secretary?
- What if I blow it or embarrass myself?
- What if they become belligerent or angry?
- What if I they think I'm intruding or pushy?
- What if the decision maker won't talk to me?
- What do I say to get them interested in what I'm offering?
- What if they ask me a question I don't know how to answer?
- What will happen to me and my family if I keep getting rejected?

While these thoughts are normal, they are also counter-productive because if you keep thinking about what might go wrong, there's an excellent chance that's exactly what will happen. That's the bad news.

The good news is that if you keep thinking about what could go right, there's an excellent chance that's exactly what will happen. And the best news of all is that you get to choose what you think about.

It doesn't matter if you have never sold before, taken a sales class or read a single book on selling; you have a core set of beliefs about what you have to do or say to get business. These beliefs form the sales process you know, are probably using now and believe should work for you, whether or not it actually does. We'll call this process the "Traditional System."

But just because you believe something is true doesn't make it true in fact; it's only true in your perception. For almost 2,000 years, people believed the earth was the center of the universe. They assumed what they saw was all there was to see and accepted that this was how the universe worked, even though they were wrong. As a business owner, you are no different if you believe:

- You have no control over how much business is out there, who may need or want what you have to offer them, or whether they'll choose you or someone else who sells the same thing.
- You have no control over what people will buy.
- You have to do specific things, say certain things and act a certain way to get potential clients to notice you, meet you or agree to work with you.
- Making a sale is a matter of luck or using manipulation or pressure.
- Your potential clients call all the shots, and all you can do is wait, hope and pray.

Whether you realize it or not, your words, thoughts, feelings and beliefs are manifesting or demonstrating in your life all the time, typically as experiences. This process is totally automatic, completely impartial and works exactly the same way for everyone all the time.

In other words, what you think about is what you bring about, literally. If you believe it is hard for you to get business, it will be hard for you to get business *because* you believe it is hard. When you believe that getting business is easy, it will be.

Thanks to this manifesting process, if you want to change your life, all you have to do is change your thinking, and your life will automatically begin to change. Unfortunately, changing your thinking is not as easy as it sounds.

In this chapter, you're beginning to learn the "Contrarian System" of selling, which will help you change the way you think about yourself and the people who will buy from you by giving you a completely different perspective on the process of selling.

But because some Contrarian System concepts may seem a bit strange at first, you may resist them. You may even get angry because they have challenged some of your long-held convictions or pushed some very sensitive buttons you didn't even know you had. Should you find yourself resisting some of these new concepts, just allow the emotions to rise and then let them go.

You're about to learn why it's so important for you to take charge of your thoughts, how you can intentionally change your negative thoughts to positive ones, and the specific actions you can take to identify and remove the internal barriers you alone are generating that are stopping your success from rushing toward you.

Go Beyond Positive Thinking

Most sales books begin with a chapter on positive thinking or having the right attitude. This is because the sales techniques they teach usually result in a great deal of frustration, anger and self-loathing, and you have to make a huge effort to get past all the problems you've created for yourself by using the techniques they've taught you.

But this chapter is included in this sales book because, thanks to the process of automatic manifestation, you get to control what demonstrations or experiences you have through your thoughts and the actions you take as a result of those thoughts. Yes, your thoughts really are things and what you think about, you bring about, whether you like it or not, whether you want it or not and whether or not it's in your best interest to have it.

As you will read, one of the main problems with the Traditional System of selling is that it fills you with fear, and fear is the biggest hurdle to your success. No, you're not going to learn how to overcome, deal with or work through your fears about selling; instead, you're going to learn a system of selling that eliminates the basis for your fears.

What you're about to read may seem far-fetched, but it's grounded in documented scientific research into the impact of consistent, positive, focused thought on the subconscious mind.[1] You'll learn that when you shift from a mindset of doubt, fear and worry and instead operate from a mindset of positive expectancy, your success is not only possible, it's inevitable.

The Power of Affirmations

The first step to changing your thinking is to be aware every time you have a negative thought or make a negative statement, and then intentionally change it to a positive thought or statement. Notice the shift in emotion from negative to positive with each of these affirmations:

Negative Affirmation	Positive Affirmation
The economy stinks.	More millionaires were made during and after the Great Depression than at any other time in our history. If they can do it then, I can do it now.
No one is buying.	Lots of people need and want what I have; all I have to do is find them.
I'll never make it.	Of course I'll be successful. That's why I started this business.
I regret I ever started this business.	I'm going to give this business everything I have. If it does go sour, I'll feel bad for a bit, but I'll be a better person for having done it.
Nothing I do to get a sale works.	I'm going to get some training and learn how to do this right.
I hate being rejected.	When people decline what I'm offering, they are not rejecting me personally. Besides, they're allowed to be wrong.

Negative Affirmation	Positive Affirmation
I hate calling on strangers.	A stranger is just someone I haven't met and gotten to know yet.
I can never get through.	Most people I call answer their own phones or return my calls shortly.
I'm charging too much.	I provide excellent value and there are plenty of people willing to pay for it.
There's too much competition.	There is more than enough business out there for everyone who wants it.
I can't afford that.	At this moment, that's not in my spending plan.

Good or bad, whatever you are saying, chances are that's exactly what you are seeing. Affirmations are extremely powerful, and you can use them to bring whatever you want into your life and keep what you don't want out of it.

Now, Not Later

Your subconscious mind doesn't know the difference between the past, present and future, so time is always "now." This is why it is extremely important to keep your affirmations in the present and not put things in the future.

When you say, *"I will have a successful business,"* you are affirming you will have a successful business someday, but since someday is in the future, your sales efforts will continuously be filled with stalls, delays and dead ends.

But when you change your affirmation to *"I now have a thriving, successful, prosperous business,"* it will begin to become yours. Own it. Feel it. Embrace and embody it. Experience it as being yours now and it will rush toward you because you manifest whatever you feel strongly about.

Always Think Positively, No Matter What

Because this process is automatic and infallible, your negative thoughts will produce negative demonstrations and your positive thoughts will produce positive demonstrations. You simply cannot have negative thoughts on a consistent basis and manifest positive experiences.

If you're complaining about something, you're focusing on precisely what you don't want, and you can expect to receive more of it. The easiest way to stop what you don't want from showing up is simply to stop complaining.

If you say, *"I hate to sell,"* you are attracting situations that will cause you to hate selling. Say instead, *"I'm really good at selling and my clients appreciate my serving them."* Say it to yourself often enough and you'll begin to feel differently about selling.

Believe It Until You See It

When you consciously, deliberately and intentionally direct your thoughts and feelings towards having–not getting–the success you desire, doors you thought were closed will open and the people you need to meet will come into your life almost magically.

You'll just happen to be in the right place at the right time, the strangest coincidences and synchronicities will occur, and from seemingly out of nowhere, golden opportunities will fall in your lap. They're simply the demonstrations of your positive beliefs.

Move Your Feet

You must do more than just affirm what you want in order to get it; you actually have to take some sort of action, and sometimes it's as simple as showing up.

> *When you know with absolute certainty what you want, take actions in alignment with your desires, completely confident that it is already yours, even if you can't yet see it.*

If you have a fledgling business and are struggling to survive, this is the time to take a leap of faith and start planning for growth. Identify what you need to do, have or know to have the kind of business you see for yourself in a few years, and then seek out the resources and/or people who can help you take your business to that next level.

While it may seem that you're being unrealistic at this early stage, just the opposite is true. If you want the picture you have in your mind to become a reality, moving in the direction of your dreams–despite the conditions you are now experiencing and other people's opinions–is the best way to do it.

Bombard Your Brain

Keep your affirmations and images of what your success looks like right in front of you so you can constantly fill your mind with the thoughts, feelings and images of having it. Turn them into screensavers, frame them around your computer, put them on your mirror, on your desktop printer and on the wall opposite your toilet, and carry them around in your wallet. You want to make sure you see them wherever you go.

Once Is Never Enough

You should say your affirmations over and over until your mind habitually carries only positive thoughts and blocks whatever negative thoughts may come up. It's like learning to touch type–you have to consciously train your fingers where to go on the keyboard so eventually they go there automatically. When you no longer have to concentrate on the process of typing, you're free to focus on the content of what you're writing.

It's the same with your thinking. To neutralize habitual negative thinking, make sure to repeat your positive affirmations at least three times a day-before you get out of bed, around lunchtime and especially right before you fall asleep, so your positive thoughts sink into your subconscious.

Do this for a while and you'll become aware when you make a negative affirmation or have a negative thought, and then you can deliberately replace it with a positive one. Because your thoughts become your experiences, when you change your thinking, you change your life.

Expect to Receive

"Ask, believe, receive" is the ancient formula for success. Once you have claimed what you want believing you have it, be grateful that you already have received it, even if it's invisible to you at the moment. When you allow what you ask for to come to you, it will rush toward you. It's really that simple.

Don't try to "make it happen." Just as you don't concern yourself with how soil turns a seed into a plant, don't concern yourself with how your belief turns into a demonstration. Your job is to know what you want, plan for it and live your life accordingly; it's the Universe's job to bring it to you.

Be a Daydream Believer

When you were a kid, you probably spent lots of time pretending you were someone, something or somewhere else. You were strong, brave, popular, rich, a movie star or astronaut, the hero or the bad guy-you could do, be or have anything you desired without limitations.

Whether you called it playing, daydreaming, fantasizing, imagining or visualizing, the effect was the same-you got to feel terrific and those feelings made you strong, happy and upbeat. They took you out of your everyday real world and into the world you created for yourself where everything worked just the way you wanted it to.

So now that you're all grown up, you can still make yourself feel great by pretending. For instance, imagine that you've just signed a major new client - you feel happy and ecstatic, and maybe even relieved and/or prosperous because of the money you'll receive. Hang on to those feelings because your subconscious mind doesn't know the difference between what you imagine and what is real.

The more you continue to be happy and ecstatic - regardless of what is happening around you - the sooner you will have experiences similar to or better than those you imagined that will cause you to be enthusiastic and ecstatic for real. That's the power of your subconscious mind.

The fastest way to manifest your success - or anything else - is to think, speak and act as if you already have it.

Chapter Three
MARKETING ISN'T SELLING

It's possible that when you opened your business, you thought that somehow clients would find you and you would never have to stoop so low as to go out and sell. While the concept of "build it and they will come" may work in the movies, the reality is that if you want business to come to you, you have to go out and get it.

But if you've never "sold," dislike the thought of pitching or hustling or are terrified of rejection, take heart. The selling you will be doing for your business is nothing like that. Selling, especially for service firms, is all about relationships, and you and your clients have to feel good about working together in order for it to work for both of you.

So how do you go about getting people-typically strangers-interested in doing business with you? You use a combination of marketing and selling. Although the terms are often used interchangeably and their joint aim is to build your bottom line, marketing and selling have several major differences:

Marketing
- Is like firing a shotgun–just blast away and you'll probably hit something
- Uses a shallow and broad approach, reaching masses of people with a generic message
- Is reactive-you hope someone will hear your message and respond to it
- Usually requires a large amount of money and a modest amount of time and energy
- Has a low to moderate potential for success over the short term

- Requires no personalized follow-up on your part
- Is based upon indirect contact with potential clients:
  - Branding your company, creating brochures and collateral material
  - Using social media
  - Networking to generate leads and referrals
  - Upgrading your website for improved SEO
  - Blogging, writing articles
  - Launching email or direct snail mail campaigns
  - Running ads
  - Holding seminars; doing public speaking, attending conferences

Selling
- Is like firing a rifle–pick out a target, evaluate the conditions, customize your approach, aim and shoot
- Uses a narrow and deep approach to reach a highly targeted clientele with a specific message unique to them
- Is proactive–you reach out to potential clients, even if they've never heard of you
- Usually requires a large amount of time and energy and a small amount of money
- Has a high potential for success in the short term
- Requires you to do personalized follow-up
- Is based upon direct contact with individuals:
  - Identifying specific clients and their interests, needs and/or opportunities
  - Contacting them one-to-one and establishing a basis for conversation
  - Meeting with them or talking on the phone
  - Addressing their questions and/or concerns
  - Preparing a proposal
  - Finalizing the sale
  - Staying in touch

> *The fundamental difference between marketing and selling is that marketing generates awareness and interest about your business among large groups of potential clients, while selling gets individual clients to say "Yes."*

Lots of commercial painters spend thousands of dollars on advertising, mailings and door hangers in the hope of attracting business, and wonder why their phone isn't ringing. But one local painter who specializes in apartments and warehouses doesn't spend a dime on marketing.

Instead, he spends three hours a day going from property to property visiting with the on-site managers. He's built his highly successful business by literally knocking on doors; he now has eight crews and is one of the busiest painters in town.

Your Business/Marketing Plan

The foundation of a successful business is a thoroughly researched and well-developed written business plan. This comprehensive document allows you to think your business concept through, identify potential problems and opportunities, and strategize actions you'll need to take before you spend any money, send off an email or pick up a phone.

> *Having a written business plan is absolutely essential to your success because it helps you clarify your vision for your business and serves as your roadmap and compass.*

Your business/marketing plan will help you determine the direction you want your business to go, and outline the best ways to get there based on real world information you will have gathered, instead of using guesswork and assumptions.

But most importantly, you will find that in the process of putting your plan together, you will answer many of the questions you didn't even know you had. This is especially true if you're starting your first or a new business, or if sales of your current business have gone flat or down and nothing you've done so far seems to be working.

Take your time and think your plan through, but don't do anything else to get business until your business plan is complete. There are numerous free websites that can take you through the process of developing your plan, including:

www.bplans.com   www.score.org

www.sba.gov   www.entrepreneur.com

The first part of a your plan will be an analysis of your business and its financials – the purpose, premise and structure of your business, as well as how much money you expect to invest in the process of making more money over a given period of time.

The second part of your plan will be an analysis of your potential clients – who they are, where they are, what they want or need and how you can best reach them. Since knowledge is power, your sales success will increase proportionately by the amount of information you have.

Marketing Plan Basics

Before you can sell anything to anybody, you have to be clear on four main points:

- What you are selling
- Who might want to buy it
- Why they might want it
- Why they might not

Your marketing plan will help you answer these questions and should include the following:

- *Mission Statement:* Why your business does what it does
- *SWOT Analysis:* Identifying your business' strengths, weaknesses, opportunities and threats
- *Target Market:* Who you are trying to reach and why they would want what you're selling
- *Competitive Analysis:* Understanding the other people who do what you do
- *Unique Selling Proposition:* What makes you different from the other people who do what you do
- *Pricing Strategy:* How much–or how little–you expect clients to pay you and why
- *Promotional Plan:* How you will reach your potential clients
- *Marketing Budget:* How much it will cost to get your message out
- *Action Plan:* What you need to do, how often and when
- *Metrics:* How you will measure the success of your marketing/sales programs

Mission Statement

Your mission statement is basically a simply-worded statement of what your business is actually about (profit motive aside) which will provide the direction and focus needed for making decisions and implementing those decisions.

This is the mission statement for my business: *"The JW Speakers Agency is the largest booking agency in the United States for local business owners who use free speaking as a way to build their business."*

Here are the mission statements of some now large companies that were once small:

Southwest Airlines: *"The mission of Southwest Airlines is dedication to the highest quality of customer service delivered with a sense of warmth, friendliness, individual pride and company spirit."*

Microsoft: *"To enable people and businesses throughout the world to realize their full potential."*

Google: *"Google's mission is to organize the world's information and make it universally accessible and useful."*

Coca-Cola: *"To refresh the world; to inspire moments of optimism and happiness; to create value and make a difference."*

There are no rules when it comes to writing your business' mission statement. You can be as specific or generic as you like, but it really comes down to answering one basic question: *"What do we do, why do we do it and who do we help?"*

SWOT Analysis

While every journey has a destination, it also has a starting point, and if you want your business to succeed, you have to be very clear about what is going on around you that affects you, your business and the lives and/or businesses of your potential clients or customers. This is where a SWOT analysis can help.

To put it simply, a SWOT analysis is a strategic planning tool that can help you identify your professional strengths and weaknesses and those of your company, and alert you to opportunities and threats that may exist in a specific situation, especially those you're not now aware of. A typical SWOT analysis will include:

- *Strengths:* What makes your business thrive
- *Weaknesses:* What your business' vulnerabilities are

- *Opportunities:* What market conditions or segments there are that can lead to growth
- *Threats:* How competitors are snapping at your heels

Here's the SWOT analysis done by a construction law firm considering offering mediation services:[2]

Strengths	*Weaknesses*
Construction law firm with staff members who are trained in both law and professional engineering/ general contracting. Small (three employees)–can change and adapt quickly.	No one at our firm has been a mediator before or been through any formal mediation training programs. One staff member has been a part of mediations, but not as a neutral party.
Opportunities	*Threats*
Most commercial construction contracts require mediation. Despite hundreds of mediators in the marketplace, only a few have actual construction experience. For smaller disputes, mediators don't work as a team, only as individuals. Our staff can offer anyone the advantage of a group of neutrals to evaluate a dispute.	Anyone can become a mediator, so other construction law firms could open up their own mediation services as well. Most potential clients think mediators don't understand or care to understand the problem and rush to resolve it.

As a result of this SWOT analysis, the partners decided to take courses and launch a new mediation division, playing on their strong name recognition and providing an extra layer of service to their clients.

Target Market

You have to have specific information about your clients in order to develop an effective strategy to reach them, including:

- Their age, sex, location, ethnicity and financial status
- Where they are located (especially critical if you want them to come to you)
- What is important to them
- What they are concerned about
- What they need, want or might be interested in having

Competitive Analysis

As you read books, articles and websites on developing your business/marketing plan, you will find there is a major emphasis on differentiating yourself from your competitors, including:

- Who and where your competitors are
- What they offer and who they serve
- What they do that is right, wrong or different from how you do the same thing
- What you see as their strengths and weaknesses compared to yours
- What may be your chances of capturing market share from them

The concept of competition is based upon the belief there is only a limited amount of business to be had and in the battle for business, it's you against them. Unfortunately, if this is what you believe, then this is what you will experience. Because what goes around comes around, if you believe someone else must lose in order for you to win, eventually you will lose.

> *Banish the idea of competition from your mind: other people who do what you do are your colleagues, and they have every right to be as successful as you are or want to be.*

The concept of lack and limitation is a myth; the truth is that there is more than enough business out there for everyone who wants it. In fact, it's standard practice for people in the same line of work to refer clients back and forth, share information or help each other grow their businesses.

Remember, what you do to or think about other people is exactly what they will do to or think about you, which is why in business, as in life, the Golden Rule rules–treat everyone the way you want to be treated and everyone will win.

Unique Selling Proposition (USP)

Your USP defines how your business is different from those of your colleagues and why that difference would make your business appealing to many of your potential clients.

> *No matter how many colleagues you have in your area, you will each have a unique selling proposition because you are all unique individuals. Your USP enables you to tailor your marketing and sales program to target those people who would be attracted to your specific business.*

At one point, I had three estate attorneys at the same time as clients in the Dallas/Fort Worth Metroplex, and while it may seem as though they might conflict with each other because they all do the same thing–wills, estate planning, elder law, probate and so on–they each had a unique selling proposition and a highly targeted clientele:

- Debbie spent many years as a single mom and was happily remarried with a houseful of children. Her market was mothers of preschoolers and working women.

- Janet was widowed at the age of 48 when her husband had a heart attack with no prior history of heart trouble. Her experience with rebuilding her life after loss inspired her to write a book on how widows can survive the death of their husbands. Her market was working adults and seniors, particular women over 50.

- Antoinette, a former attorney/legal advisor for the U.S. Army in her 40s, focused her practice on families with special needs, Medicaid and veterans benefits.

Pricing Strategy

How much should you charge? It all depends on what you're selling, how you're selling it to whom, and most importantly, how much value they place on what they're buying. If you have other colleagues in your area, you should have a good idea of their going rate.

Your potential clients will perceive your value to them based upon your unique selling proposition, and it's your value-not your cost-that matters. You must believe you're worth what you're charging, otherwise no one else will.

Years ago, I was a very successful commercial real estate writer and publicist, and in addition to writing for national trade publications under my own byline, I did a lot of ghostwriting for clients for these magazines. Since I had no learning curve about the industry and was a professional writer, at least 95% of the time, I got at least 95% of what they wanted on the first draft.

Often, these commercial real estate companies had used general business or consumer-oriented public relations or marketing agencies before and were astonished that my work required little or no rewriting. Because my value to them was so high, my fees were much higher than general PR/marketing firms, and no one ever complained about the price.

It was a win-win-win arrangement: each client got a well-written article published in a leading national trade magazine that his colleagues thought he had written, the magazine got a well-researched and professionally-written article which required no editing, and I got the check.

Marketing Mix

After you have determined who you want to reach, where they are and what they want to have, be or know, it's now time to select the most cost-effective ways to reach them, such as:

- Website marketing/SEO
- Email marketing/e-zine (e-newsletter)
- Public speaking
- Publicity
- Article writing/blogging
- Networking
- Advertising
- Social media

How should you allocate your marketing dollars? Well, if you're not on the web and not on the first or second pages of Google when someone does a search for what you're providing, you can't expect too many people to find you. Most people won't search past the first few pages of Google, and if your site isn't there, it might as well be invisible.

Clearly, your biggest initial marketing expense will be your website and the costs associated with search engine optimization (SEO). Don't stint here; hire the best talent you can afford at this point; you can always upgrade and/or revise your site when you have a stronger cash flow. What's left over of your marketing budget can be easily stretched to cover anything else.

Spending Smart

There are lots of websites on low-cost marketing strategies you can do yourself, and plenty of providers in your area who can provide such services. If you're really strapped for cash, offer your company as a case study for a college marketing class project or hire a student majoring in public relations or marketing who can give you a few hours a week at dirt cheap rates.

You can also take advantage of the talent that surrounds you. Several years ago when I was selling patient care equipment, I attended the home health industry's annual trade show and met a manufacturer of van lifts for scooters and wheelchairs who needed a name for a new lift.

Instead of paying an advertising agency thousands of dollars, he ran a contest for the trade show attendees – name the lift and you win $100 and a plaque. His manual wheelchair lift was called "The Caddy," so I came up with "The Backpack." Shortly thereafter, the manufacturer selected my entry as the winner, and while I was very happy to get the check, I never did get that plaque.

Splash vs. Drip Marketing

Let's say you want to spread the word about your company in a big way. You hire a public relations/marketing agency and they do a great job of getting you out there in the media and on the web, branded to the hilt. You're famous, you have a savvy new website and you get your 15 minutes of fame in ads, YouTube, radio and television appearances and so on.

This is the "splash" method of marketing–a lot of activity done in a short period of time that typically costs a whole lot of money. The problem with splash marketing is that shortly after the agency stops working for you, all the hoopla they've created fades away real fast and you're now left on your own to keep that momentum going.

When it comes to small local businesses, a better tactic is the "drip" method of marketing–a little bit of activity done consistently over a long period of time. Not only are the costs of drip marketing a fraction of the cost of splash marketing, the results can be astounding and long-lasting. Here's what a typical drip marketing program might look like over the course of a year:

- Website marketing/SEO–ongoing and automatic
- Email marketing/e-zine (e-newsletter)–once a week or every two weeks
- Public speaking–twice a month
- Print/radio publicity–once a month
- Article writing/blogging–once a month
- Networking with local groups–twice a month minimum
- Advertising–as needed or none at all
- Social media–on-going in appropriate outlets

If you use email marketing, much of your writing can be done well ahead of time, and all email services allow you to schedule your emails or e-zines weeks or months in advance.

Getting Publicity

In terms of publicity, there are many free or low cost sites where you can post articles and issue press releases, but the most effective way to get publicity is to develop your own media list and send your material directly to relevant reporters, writers and editors, especially those right in your area.

If you're an expert and especially if you've written a book, which automatically makes you an expert, contact the hosts of the radio talk shows on your local stations because they're always looking for interesting topics to bring to their listeners. And don't forget internet radio talk shows like BlogTalkRadio.com where you can host your own show and be a guest on other people's shows. Many of these online radio shows are free or low cost.

Getting publicity on the web is typically done by getting bloggers to include you in their posts, much like reporters including you in their stories. The best way to reach bloggers is through their feedback form; just make sure that what you write to them is relevant to their content and the people they reach.

Public Speaking

I admit I'm biased, but as an old-fashioned, off-line B2B publicist, I believe the most cost-effective way for a local service business to generate clients is through public speaking. This is free speaking where you don't get paid to speak, but instead share a bit about what you know with groups of people who are interested in what you have to say, and you get paid by getting business as a result of your speaking.

The best way to start speaking is to develop a list of groups relevant to your business, such as Rotary, Kiwanis and Lions clubs, moms groups, women's groups, senior groups, business groups, Chambers of Commerce and trade associations. Everything you need is on the internet; just start searching through Google.

You'll typically find contact information for the club president and/or program chair on the group's website; if it's not there, Google the person's name and use an online White Pages directory to get their home number, if necessary.

People who are active in one community or business group tend to be active in others, so chances are good that if you look hard enough, you find their phone and/or email.

Now pick up the phone, talk to the club president or program chair and send an email that contains a summary of your talk and what the group's members will learn or experience from it. A week or so later or whenever they tell you to, call back and arrange your speaking date.

Of course, if you don't want to be bothered doing all this yourself, you can have someone do it for you, such as your assistant, a college student or a booking firm like The JW Speakers Agency.

A Model Marketing Plan

Let's say you are a tax accountant and want to reach out to local business owners within a 30-mile radius of your town. Your ideal clients:

- Are college-educated, highly-experienced professionals or drop-outs from Corporate America who now have their own businesses
- Have between five and 20 employees
- Probably use a bookkeeper for day-to-day record-keeping and/or an accountant who prepares financial statements, but neither is a tax specialist
- May have been audited or received a friendly letter from the IRS or they are concerned either or both could happen
- Usually pay more taxes than they need to but don't realize it

Armed with this information, you know that your customers can best be reached by:

- Having a professionally-designed and fully optimized website and blogging and/or writing articles for the web that link back to your site
- Speaking at Chambers of Commerce, service clubs, business groups and trade associations in your area
- Writing for your local weekly business journal

- Advertising in your Chambers of Commerce's online and offline directories and on their websites and perhaps sponsoring some of their events
- Being an expert guest on local radio talk shows, especially around tax season
- Networking at local business events, monthly Chamber meetings and trade association meetings

---

*Splash marketing is done **to** you, reaches masses of people whose potential interest is unknown, is artificially created and usually generates short-lived results.*

---

*Drip marketing is done **through** you, reaches a limited number of people whose potential interest is strong, reflects your business' personality and usually generates long-lasting results.*

Timing the Results

How long will it take for you to see results from your investment in marketing? A good rule of thumb is that if you put together a drip marketing program like the one outlined above, you should begin to see results within six months.

Usually between six and 18 months, a snowball effect comes into effect as you generate word-of-mouth advertising, which is the very best kind. People you never heard of start contacting you, colleagues begin to refer clients they can't help or don't want, you're suddenly known as an expert in your field, and you're amazed how all this new business seemed to come out of nowhere.

A Word of Caution

If this is your first business, you may have unrealistic expectations about how much business your marketing will generate, especially at first. Remember, marketing's role is to develop awareness about your business, but awareness doesn't pay the bills.

Until you are already well known in your community as an expert and people are coming to you, you're going to have to go out and get the business yourself. And even after you are well known in your community as an expert and people are coming to you, you're still going to have to go out and get more business in order to ensure the business keeps coming to you.

This is called selling.

Chapter Four
GETTING READY TO SELL

You've done your business plan and are working on developing the right mindset, but you're still not ready to go out and sell. Before you pick up the phone or write an email, you need to have the right tools; otherwise you'll be running your business like an unpaid hobby instead of a profitable business.

Customer Relationship Management (CRM) Program

It's 2:30 PM on a busy Tuesday and the phone rings. *"Hi, it's Sam and I'm returning your call."* the voice says. You know you know someone named Sam, but can't remember who he is, what company he's with, what you called him about or when you called him.

Fortunately, you have a customer relationship management (CRM) system in place and within seconds, you've found the right Sam in your database and scanned your notes you made during your previous conversations with him.

"Hi, Sam," you say. *"Thanks so much for getting back to me. The last time we spoke, you suggested..."* As the two of you talk, you make notes in Sam's contact file, schedule a follow-up call and send him an email which is automatically copied into his file in your database.

Thanks to your CRM program, you have taken care of business quickly and effortlessly and made an indelible impression on Sam–and everyone else you deal with–that you are efficient, polished and professional which, of course, you are.

Just as its name implies, a CRM manages all the various interactions between you and everyone who is important to your business–your employees or contractors and your leads, potential and current clients or customers, vendors, associates, resources and colleagues.

Each CRM system is different, but most track various inbound and outbound communications, automate sales activities and manage marketing activities. Four of the most popular programs include ACT!, Goldmine, Salesforce and Infusionsoft.

Whether you want a single-user CRM program that is downloaded to your computer or a cloud-based program for multiple users, be sure to compare various programs for their functions, features, pricing, flexibility, ease of use and integration capabilities with other software, especially your email provider.

All CRM programs allow you to create and manage a comprehensive customer database and update it with notes, meeting schedules, documents and other pertinent information, and integrate your database with email and social media marketing campaigns.

More sophisticated programs allow you to analyze sales, develop reports, forecast future sales and integrate your database with online accounting software like QuickBooks and email marketing software like Constant Contact.

Regardless of the nature of your business or the size of your budget, there is a CRM program just right for you. Given all the advantages they offer your business, there's no reason not to use one.

Email Services

While you have to have email these days, you also have to use the email service that is right for your business. The following guide provides an overview of the four most popular small business email services (2013 prices shown):[3]

Outlook

Price: $109.95 (suggested retail)
Operating System: Windows

Outlook, the most popular email client for business, is available as a standalone or as part of the Microsoft Office Suite which retails for around $400. Outlook lets you organize and filter messages easily and integrate email easily with scheduling and to-do lists. On the downside, it does take a little effort to set up and it can be a bit sluggish.

Outlook is also available with Business Contact Manager which provides basic CRM features like project management and sales pipelines, and you can even import contacts from other programs like ACT!

Mail

Price: Free with Mac OS X
Operating System: Mac OS X

Apple's Mail comes built-in with all-Mac operating systems and has many of the same features as Outlook. It works with most POP and IMAP standards, so you can view your Yahoo!, Gmail or Hotmail email. Mail is really three programs in one: Mail, iCal and Address Book and is relatively easy to set up and use.

Thunderbird

Price: Free
Operating System: Mac OS X, Windows, Linux

Thunderbird is Mozilla's open source email client and uses the tabs that have made Mozilla's Firefox browser so popular. You can open emails in tabs and jump between them the same way you do in Firefox.

Thunderbird's time line tool also lets you find what you're looking for faster. You can customize with smart folders and Mozilla's famous add-ons, including Lightning which integrated the Sunbird calendar.

Gmail

Price: Free
Operating System: Not Applicable

Google's web-based Gmail allows you to manage your email from any computer or smart phone. Gmail doesn't use folders, which can take some getting used to. Instead, users attach labels and emails are grouped into threaded conversations.

Gmail offers a robust search and lots of other features including integration with Google Docs, Calendar and Chat. Like Mozilla's add-ons, you can enable Google Labs to experiment with new features. You can access all of your mail accounts from one Gmail account and even display them simultaneously as unique mailboxes.

Action Plan

In your marketing plan, you outlined in general terms who your potential clients are and how you expect to reach them. Now in your action plan, you will define the precise steps you're going to take over a specific period of time, how much time and/or money you expect to invest and what you realistically expect to achieve as a result of your actions.

By developing a written action plan, you will translate your big ideas into concrete reality and start moving in the direction of your dreams. After all, unless you know where you're going, you can't expect to get anywhere. Start by clearly defining what you want to achieve; steer clear of generalities; your goal should be SMART: specific, measurable, achievable, realistic and timely.

Let's say you're a CPA who wants to shift your practice from working with individuals to doing accounting for local small and medium-sized businesses. Your goal is to secure at least ten new clients within the next 12 months with a minimum monthly billing of $2,000 each, and this is the action plan you've developed:

- You join the local bar association as an affiliate member and attend the monthly meetings in order to generate referrals from attorneys, most of whom have their own small practices.
  You meet one-on-one with at least two different attorneys a month and take the same approach with financial planners, investment advisors and bankers.

- You network directly with your potential clients by joining the local Chamber of Commerce and attending at least one networking function a month.

- You contact the editor of your local business journal and offer to write a monthly column or contribute articles on a quarterly basis.

- If you're not already doing so, you keep in touch with your past, current and pending clients with an email newsletter every week or every two weeks that shares relevant, timely information they can use.

- You schedule yourself at least two speaking engagements a month with local Rotary Clubs, business groups, trade associations and/or Chambers of Commerce.

- You develop a talk for attorneys and invest the time and effort to have it approved for continuing legal education credits so you can speak before the local bar associations and give lunch 'n learns at large law firms in your area.

- You put together a PDF called, "What You Need to Know About Business Taxes" to use as an incentive for people to sign up for your e-newsletter on your website and at your speaking engagements.

- You hold a roundtable lunch at your office with a different group of local business owners each quarter, always ensuring that an attorney and banker/financial advisor are invited.

The only part of this program that costs you money is membership in the Chamber of Commerce and bar Association fees and the sandwiches for the lunch 'n learns and workshops, but you'll easily recoup those tax-deductible marketing costs with the first client you pick up.

Your Online Image

Before the Internet existed, any company worth its salt had a printed brochure, but now if you want to be found, you have to be online. Just having a website–even one that's optimized–isn't enough; your site must project the kind of image you want your company to have.

Your potential clients will form a judgment about your professional capabilities and decide whether or not to do business with you based upon the impression your website makes.

Take a good, hard look at your website and then check out the sites of your most successful colleagues. If your site could use a makeover, find a good website designer to give it an overhaul and increase its optimization so it appears on the first page of Google when people search for your services or products.

But don't stop there—make sure you use an email address with your website as its domain, instead of using Gmail, AOL, Yahoo or other consumer-oriented email address. Your website designer can arrange this for you and it will make a tremendous difference in the way you and your business are perceived.

The Sales Cycle

The sales cycle is a distinct sequence of steps a typical client goes through when deciding to buy something. There are a lot of variables, but most sales include most of these steps:

- *Prospecting/Qualifying:* You find potential clients that broadly meet your criteria and determine if they have the need, interest, desire and resources to buy what you're offering, and move the conversation forward

- *Getting Together*: You meet or talk at least once with your potential clients to see if there is synergy between you, discuss their needs and provide details on your services

- *Addressing Their Concerns:* They will have questions, and you should be ready with the answers

- *Finalizing the Deal:* You and they agree to do business together

We will deal with each stage of the sales cycle in depth in the following chapters.

Part 2:
PROSPECTING/QUALIFYING

Chapter Five
PROSPECTING/QUALIFYING BASICS

In this initial stage of selling, your potential clients will fall into one of these categories:

- *Hot Leads*: These potential clients know enough about you and your products or services to begin exploring how you can work together

- *Warm Leads*: These potential clients have heard of you either through referrals or marketing, know something about your products or services and want to know more

- *Cold Calls*: These potential clients don't yet know you and need to be educated about why they should care about what you have to offer them

Hot Leads

It couldn't be better – you have an interested potential client on the phone, in your inbox or right in front of you, and now it's just a matter of seeing if there's a fit between what you have, what they really want, can afford and are ready to purchase.

If you're just starting out in business or are scrambling for clients, it's very tempting to take on anyone who's willing to pay you. But if you don't set guidelines, you may find yourself with clients who default, go out of business or simply go poof.

To save yourself a lot of grief, decide precisely the kind of clients you want to have, the terms of your working relationship with them and how you expect to be compensated for your services or products. If you pursue and accept only those clients who meet your criteria, you'll create your own niche, put yourself in demand and ensure your success.

Warm Leads

You probably think it would be wonderful to have a business built on referrals so you won't have to go out and sell. After all, word of mouth is the best form of advertising and who better to recruit new clients for you than people you already do business with?

There are lots of so-called "referral generating systems" on the web that promise to share secrets no one else knows that will turn your contacts into your own salesforce and have new clients banging down your door because you will be irresistible to them.

No need to spend the money on someone else's system; just create your own. All you have to do is provide the best service or product for the most value, treat your current clients and referral sources like gold, and do it over and over and over. They'll automatically spread the word.

What matters most is the quality of the referrals you get; not the quantity.

Referral Resources

Here are some ways for you to help yourself get referrals:

- *Create an alliance of complementary providers*: As a booking agent, I frequently get requests for virtual assistants, speech coaches, website designers and agents for professional speakers. I don't get referral fees from these vendors, but the good will I generate from my introductions to them more than makes up for the petty cash.

- *Thank those who refer you*: Don't just send a thank you email or card; follow-up with the person who made the referral and let them know how it all worked out.

- *Offer an incentive*: One accounting firm offers a 100% refund on its fees–each current client gets four cards; for each one that comes back through a new client, the current clients get 25% off, up to 100%.

   All of my clients receive one free booking for every referral they make who becomes a client of The JW Speakers Agency. There is no limit as to how many free bookings clients can receive through their referrals.

- *Offer incentives among your staff*: Encourage those who work for or with you to make referrals by offering gifts, awards, bonuses, lump payments or a percentage of what the client bills.

- *Have a referral contest*: A chiropractor I know holds a contest each year in which he encourages his patients to make referrals. The prize for the most referrals over the course of that month is a weekend for two at a local resort. The cost of the getaway is tax deductible to the chiropractor.

- *Have legitimate testimonials on your website*: Having a few lines from "Mary S., Healthcare Executive" is worse than having nothing at all. If you don't have any testimonials, ask your current clients for some.

- *Keep your clients and referral sources up-to-date*: Chances are those you do business with and/or your professional colleagues have

PROSPECTING/QUALIFYING BASICS

a limited understanding of the services you provide. Tell them what else you do and suggest ways you can help them.

- *Hold "by invitation only" lunches*: Invite half a dozen potential clients, vendors, suppliers and referral sources whose businesses complement each other to a lunch, over which they can discuss a topic of interest to them all. For the price of lunch, you'll make several new friends, most if not all of whom will become your clients and/or your biggest fans.

- *Be a catalyst for change:* A local business bank holds an annual party for its small business clients, most of whom haven't met each other before. Another bank sponsors a group for local women business owners and underwrites an internship/mentoring program for female college students.

- *Make your clients feel great about you*: One particular house painter does just as good a job as every other house painter and his rates are just as competitive, but he has more business than he can handle.

    When the job is done, he leaves the homeowner (typically the wife) a thank you note and a flower pot. He calls a week later to see how she likes the paint job and asks if any of her friends could use their house painted. He typically comes away from that call with referrals, and as she tells all her friends about him, his phone starts ringing.

- *Get endorsed*: Let's say you provide website design services for contractors. You find the local chapters of the various contractor trade associations and contact the presidents, offering to revamp the group's website in exchange for an endorsement letter you can use to market to their membership.

- *Ask for referrals*: If you've provided great service and your clients are happy, ask them to tell their friends and colleagues. Most will do it automatically; you just won't know about it until later.

The Referral Trap

All that said, there is a downside to having a business built on referrals. In 1987, I got laid off from my job as the director of public relations for New York-based Landauer Associates, the country's premier commercial real estate valuation and consulting firm. If you were a corporation, financial institution, pension fund, insurance company or private owner with an unusual real estate need, you came to Landauer.

Since I was going to start my own commercial real estate public relations agency, I had lunch with the owner of Landauer's advertising agency in order to pick his brain. Then in his late '60s, Art had built up the company his father started 40 years earlier to become the largest and most prestigious commercial real estate advertising and public relations agency in New York City.

This was the peak of the bull market in the biggest commercial real estate market in the world, and Art represented most of the major industry players in the city. Naively, I asked Art how he recruited clients and he said smugly, *"I don't go out and get clients; they come to me."*

Now, most people would be very impressed and wish they were in Art's shoes, but I was appalled. Art, who I thought was a savvy and street-smart business owner, had fallen into the trap of relying on referrals as the backbone of his business.

In his opinion, business was booming and there was no reason to think anything would change. But actually, there was plenty of reason to think that. Yes, we were in a bull market and the New York commercial real estate market was growing like crazy, but the handwriting was already on the wall that the end was in sight. Unfortunately, Art couldn't or wouldn't see it.

In the mid-1980s when interest rates went into double digits, savings and loans defaulted en masse and the empty office, retail, industrial and hotel buildings they had invested in around the country littered the skyline. As the banks failed, property values plummeted in Texas and elsewhere; a real estate crisis in Manhattan was inevitable.

I wasn't the only one who saw it coming. The handful of other commercial real estate advertising and PR agencies in Manhattan began to quietly diversify in order to cushion the blow when the bottom fell out. I wondered what Art would do when business stopped walking in the door, and I didn't have to wonder for long.

When the New York City real estate crash hit in late 1989, I was saddened but not surprised that Art's business crumbled with it. He told me that one of his now-bankrupt clients owed him $250,000, and within six months, Art went from having 25 employees to two. He finally went out of business and took a job with one of those other advertising/PR agencies.

If you lose or fail to develop the ability to go out and get business, you lose control over the future of your business.

Giving and Getting Referrals

One of the great laws of the Universe is whatever you give to others, you get back multiplied. So if you want more referrals, make more referrals, but make sure they're good ones. Think about the last time you made a referral to someone. Were you just passing along a contact or actually endorsing them? How much of yourself did you put on the line?

Many entrepreneurs swear by leads groups, and while they definitely work for some types of local businesses, relying on other people to feed you leads or make referrals to you can make you passive. A better approach is to consider referrals a bonus – celebrate when they happen, but don't rely on them to pay your bills on a consistent basis.

Generating Leads

In addition to all the networking, referrals and marketing activity you can do, you have a wealth of resources right in front of you to find people who might be interested in what you're selling:

- *Websites, blogs, newsfeeds, etc.*: Just type in a few words in Google, and you'll pull up thousands of sites, lots of e-zines to subscribe to and tons of free downloads.

- *Publications and directories*: The internet is great, but don't forget what's printed. Most of what you'll need is on the web or at your local library.

- *Industry magazines*: There's no better way to keep up with what's going on, what companies are doing what, and who the players are than by reading the trades. Many, if not most, of these are also online.

- *Annual directories or buyer's guides*: Most trade and business magazines publish annual guides which can be invaluable sources of information.

- *Chambers of Commerce and trade associations*: These organizations typically have regular membership meetings, networking functions and lunch 'n learns, not to mention their membership directory online. If you are not already a member of your local Chamber and/or trade association, make the investment and join up.

- *Trade show exhibitor lists*: Go to the show's website and you'll find out who was there and who you missed if you didn't go.

- *White and yellow pages websites*: Better than the phone book, these websites allow you to search by keyword, industry and distance from your home. Be warned: just because information is on the web doesn't mean it is accurate or current.

- *Your daily newspaper*: The news, metro and business sections will tell you what is happening in your own town where most of your potential clients are.

- *Your local or regional business newspaper*: These publications are gold mines of information, especially their annual Book of Lists, which comes free with your subscription, but is also available in the reference section of your local library.

- *What's all around you:* Let's say you're a horse lover and have been riding for years. You've just started up a business providing consulting services to equestrian professionals, but you need a way to find companies in the horse business.

    You actually have an overload of resources – start with Google, and then add in the people and companies written about and advertising in the riding and breeding magazines you're already reading, those who sponsor the stock shows and participate at industry events you attend, and those whose products you now use on your own horses.

    Even though these companies are an intricate part of your world as a horse lover, it may not have occurred to you that they could be potential clients. They're reaching out to you every way they can; all you have to do is reach back to them.

- *Everyone you know in your industry and those you don't:* Talk to your ex-fellow employees, ex-bosses and buddies, and reach out to those you don't know or don't know well, such as your present or previous clients, suppliers or vendors, and especially your colleagues at other companies.

You will be amazed how helpful people in your industry will be, and their suggestions can lead you in new directions and open doors you didn't even know existed. You see, you're a new source of information and contacts for them as well.

- *Industry groups:* Regardless of the business you're in, there's bound to be a local chapter in your area that meets on a regular basis that you can join. Here's where colleagues in the same industry meet, greet, network and share information.

  If you're new to a group, don't let the fact that you don't know anyone there yet stop you. Just walk up to someone, stick out your hand and say, *"Hi, I'm..."* The first meeting is the hardest, but at the second meeting, you're seeing familiar faces and by the third meeting, you are a familiar face.

  Trade groups are essential for keeping up with industry trends, not only because of the peer networking but because of the presentations and presenters. You will learn things that don't appear in the trade magazines and business press and you will make connections that otherwise may never have happened.

  You can find these groups by asking people in your industry, checking at your library for a directory of associations or by going to such sites as www.weddles.com, and reading the magazines in the reception areas of the companies you visit. Then get your own subscriptions.

  When you do a Google search for your industry, you'll pull up trade organizations where you'll find information on your local chapter; then just show up at the next meeting. You'll be surprised how quickly you'll be considered one of them.

> *Regularly mingle with people with whom you want to do business and/or be affiliated because they are your potential friends, clients and colleagues. You'll get to know them and they'll get to know you, and together you'll discover ways to help each other.*

Cold Calls

Cold calling-contacting potential customers who don't yet know you, may never have heard of you and have no idea why they should be interested in what you have to offer-is usually the most dreaded and feared aspect of selling.

There's a common Traditional System belief that cold calling is emotionally demanding because some people you call could be verbally abusive, some won't even bother to talk to you and hang up, while others will simply say, *"no."*

I heard one sales trainer state that since 98% of cold calls will result in *"no,"* the best you can do is to get used to it, expect it and don't take it personally. Here's what's wrong with Traditional System cold callers:

- They know and care nothing about you and have no idea why you would want, need or be interested in their product or service
- Their call is an unwelcome interruption
- They pitch, are obviously reading a script and won't let you get a word in edgewise
- They are unintelligible, can't or won't answer questions and know little or nothing about the product or service they want you to buy

No wonder 98% of these calls are wasted! Traditional System cold calling, like junk mail and email blasts, is simply another form of shotgun marketing-blindly shooting away and hoping for the best.

Selling is most definitely a numbers game because the more people you talk to, the greater your chances of making a sale. But the key is not how many calls you make, but rather how many of those calls result in a positive outcome.

The solution to shotgun cold calling is to use the rifle approach—learn as much as you can about the people and/or companies you're calling, and before you pick up the phone or send an email, use your common sense and knowledge about them to determine why they would want what you have. In the next chapter, you'll learn how to turn cold calls into warm leads by doing it right.

Chapter Six
QUALIFYING MR. BIGG

At this point, you should have a large list of potential clients, and now it's time to qualify them. Not everybody who could be a client will be one, but among the many people you haven't yet talked to, there are plenty who might be, if you handle your "First Contact" with them properly.

First Contact is just what it sounds like–your very first "touch" with a potential client–whether it's in person, on the phone or by email or letter. When it's done right, First Contact can be a golden opportunity to turn strangers into clients and/or referral sources, but when it's done wrong, you'll never get another chance to make a good impression.

Here's where you use the information you gathered for your business plan about your potential clients – who they are, what they want, need or are interested in and how you might help them. Qualifying your potential clients identifies those who do and don't meet your criteria and lays the groundwork for a good relationship between the two of you.

Before you make First Contact, you need to have specific information about your potential client, who we will call "John Bigg," to know if there's a potential match between what he may want or need and what you have to offer him:

- *Who the real Mr. Bigg is:* Mr. Bigg is the person who has the authority to buy from you. In B2B sales, this could be a purchasing person, division executive, office manager or company owner. In B2C selling situations, Mr. Bigg could be an individual, couple, parent or significant other.

When I was at Landauer, Mr. Bigg was my boss, the company's chief administrative officer. But in reality, anyone who wanted to sell any kind of marketing or advertising services to us had to go through me first, so I was also Mr. Bigg.

I had the ability to say *"no"* and the authority to say *"maybe,"* and I sat through a lot of very bad sales presentations. Only one sales rep got my blessing and actually saw my boss, and while he didn't get the sale, all those other salespeople never even got a chance.

- *What he is using now*: I recently got a phone call from a home security systems vendor. After determining I owned a home, the sales rep's next question was, *"Have you heard about our new Excel Home Security System?"*

  That was the wrong way to begin First Contact because it was clear his call was really about his product and not my home. If the sales rep had wanted this phone call to last more than the ten seconds it did, his first question should have been something like, *"Do you have a home security system in place?"*

  That question would have led to a conversation about my possible concern for my security and my possible interest in having a home security system, possibly leading to him securing an appointment for an on-site evaluation, which is the reason he called me in the first place.

  If you're selling mobile technology, don't ask if Mr. Bigg already has a smartphone–just about everyone does these days, so that question would be bordering on the ridiculous and you would look foolish.

  Since mobile technology is becoming increasingly sophisticated, you would want to determine whether and how much interest in and/or need and/or desire Mr. Bigg has for the features and benefits of your particular devices by asking such questions as, *"What mobile devices are you now using? How long ago did you buy them? How are you using your mobile devices in your business?"*

- *How Mr. Bigg feels about his current product*: Once you know what Mr. Bigg is using, you now want to learn how he feels about it. Chances are his current product has good and bad points, and if you have a product that does something better than what he is already using, you'll have a good chance of getting a fair hearing.

    Back to the mobile device example, you would ask questions like, *"What would you like your mobile devices to do that they're not currently doing for you? What features do you use the most and the least? Are your devices bigger or smaller than you'd like?"*

- *Can he switch now*: While you want to make the sale now and assuming Mr. Bigg may want it now, there may be lots of other factors causing him to wait, and money is usually the big one. You need to make sure he can afford what you're selling and if you're providing an on-going service, you need to make sure he will continue to be able to afford it.

    I learned the hard way that while new business owners are often eager to use public speaking to get clients, they're typically not a fit for my booking agency because it may take a couple of years before they can generate sufficiently steady cash flow to be able to afford us on a regular, consistent basis.

    Established businesses, especially larger ones, have different money concerns, since they often allocate their funds tightly and plan their purchases to fit their annual budgets. A good rule of thumb is that the higher your price tag, the more complicated the sale will be and the longer it may take to close the deal.

    Another possibility is that Mr. Bigg may have a contract with another provider and he needs to wait until his obligation is fulfilled, or that another Mr. Bigg in the decision-making process is unavailable. In either situation, the best qualifying question you can ask when Mr. Bigg stalls is, *"What does your timeframe look like?"*

- *When you need to walk away*: There has to be a fit between what you have to offer and what Mr. Bigg wants or needs, and if there isn't, say so; Mr. Bigg will appreciate your honesty.

   When you graciously back away from Mr. Bigg, you open the door for referrals by asking, *"Even though what I have may not work for you, do you know someone else who might benefit from it?"* Don't be surprised if he says "yes."

Chapter Seven
FIRST CONTACT: BY PHONE

How do you prefer to be approached by someone who wants to sell you something–by phone, text, email, snail mail or in person? The answer is, of course, it all depends–on your personality, what's happening in your life and business at that moment, what is being sold and by whom.

Since you're contacting Mr. Bigg who, based upon your research, you have identified as being a likely candidate for your products or services, there's a strong possibility he will react favorably when you approach him. There is also a strong possibility he has no need for or interest in what you're selling and/or doesn't want to be bothered. But you'll never know until you try.

Depending upon your personal preference, you may decide to ease into cold calling by sending an email first or you may be the adventurous type and dive right in by calling first. Both ways are right and both ways work, if you work them correctly. We'll deal with phone calls in this chapter and emails/letters in the next.

Traditional System Phone Calls

You're all ready to pick up the phone, but what do you say to a total stranger that will make him or her want to buy? The Traditional System has plenty of advice for you:[4]

- *Get their attention in 15 seconds or less: That's how long you have before your prospect realizes this is just another lousy sales call and stops listening to you.*

- *Create excitement: Think yourself into this mindset: you have a fantastic product that will make a great improvement in your customer's life. You're about to give the person on the other end of the line a huge present by telling them about this wonderful product. Then make sure that energy and enthusiasm comes across in your tone of voice.*

- *Mirror the prospect: People are most comfortable dealing with other people who are like them. Jot down a few words or phrases that your prospect uses and work them into your pitch. Try to match their volume, speed and tone of voice as well (without taking it to the point of caricature).*

- *Use their favorite word: Since a person's favorite word is their own name, write it down and then use it at least three times during the call.*

- *Don't take "no" for an answer: Many prospects will reflexively say "I'm not interested" or "I'm busy" without really hearing what you have to offer. Instead of hanging up, try asking an open-ended question to jump-start the conversation, such as "What is your biggest problem right now?" or "What are your goals?"*

- *Use emotion: Benefits sell because they inspire emotion in your prospect: happy feelings about having your product, bad feelings about not having it. Storytelling is very effective, so toss in an anecdote or two about your customers and how your product improved their lives.*

- *Provide value: Offer the prospect something useful whether or not they buy your product. This can range from a free sample to a no-strings-attached trial period. Giving something valuable to your prospect creates the feeling they "owe" you.*

- *Close every prospect: If the prospect won't talk, ask about a better time to call back. If you get a chance to make your phone pitch, ask when you can come over to make a full presentation. Close every single call, even if the prospect seems completely uninterested. You really have nothing to lose and a lot to gain by making the attempt.*

On the contrary, you have plenty to lose by making these kinds of phone calls – a lot of time, a great deal of energy and a good chunk of your confidence in your ability to make things happen.

It's essential to remember that you and Mr. Bigg are the same person – what you feel when you get a Traditional System phone call is precisely what he feels when you make such a call to him. He'll know in a heartbeat that he's being pitched, and it will become very clear to you very quickly that closing someone who seems completely uninterested is pointless.

If you want to change the way Mr. Bigg responds to your phone calls, you need to change the way you think about him, what you are saying to him and how you want him to feel about you when you say it.

Contrarian System Phone Calls

By now, you should have quite a sizeable list of Mr. Biggs to call on, but since you're going for the quality, not quantity, of calls, your contact list should be culled to include only those individuals or people inside specific companies who, from what you know about them, might be good candidates for you to approach.

Doing your homework is essential, especially if you're selling business to business. Even a cursory web search will unearth a wealth of information about each company and their industry: what they do, sell or make for whom and why; the size and nature of their operation; the location of their offices and/or facilities; their position in the marketplace, and some key contacts who may or may not be relevant to you.

Do not assume any of this information is accurate or current, but use it as a starting point. Companies are constantly changing: they are growing, shrinking, opening, closing, merging, moving, buying, selling, adding or dropping lines of business, hiring, firing, retiring, promoting people and restructuring themselves.

This is why information you have gathered may be outdated by the time you see it, especially anything off the internet. Many company websites are updated infrequently at best and are often unreliable and inaccurate. The only way to know if you have current, accurate information is to call the company.

If you're selling to corporations, ask the receptionist for the name and title of the person in charge of the department you need to contact; this is your Mr. Bigg. If you're selling to individuals or other small companies, chances are that the contact information on their website is correct and Mr. Bigg is the owner.

Mr. Bigg is the only person you should deal with because he is the only one who has the authority to say "yes." Everyone else you will encounter–secretaries, receptionists or other employees–have the ability to say "no," but they have no authority to say "yes."

Calling Big Companies

You've just developed a new app ideal for mobile sales forces and have targeted corporations as potential clients, but before you can reach Mr. Bigg, you have to get past the receptionist:

Receptionist: *"Ajax Industries. How may I direct your call?"*
You: *"Um, yes. I'm trying to get the name of the person in charge of your sales department, please."*

Receptionist: *"I can't give out that information"* or *"Who's calling?"* or *"Is he expecting your call?"*

You don't know what to say, so you mumble something about calling back later and then hang up. The infamous gatekeeper has won again. Why do they make it so hard to get through?

The receptionist's job is to greet people who do business with her company and direct their calls, not to pass judgment on them. She has absolutely no authority, can't speak for her boss or company and doesn't make buying decisions.

Never tell the receptionist why you are calling; if she asks intrusive or interrogating questions, simply pretend you didn't hear her; it really is none of her business. For all she knows, you are a major customer who is thoroughly insulted at being grilled by an insubordinate clerical worker.

So, if the receptionist starts to interrogate you, pause, smile at her audacity and say it like you mean it: *"I need some information about your CRM system. Please transfer me to your sales director."* Your confident manner and expectation you will be put through ensures that you will.

Calling Small Companies

Now let's assume you've adapted your new app for small business owners and you want to start making sales in your own area with specific companies. You could go to their websites and get an idea of who they are and what they do, but you want more than sales; you want relationships that will lead to additional referrals, contacts and those precious word-of-mouth endorsements down the road.

Armed with basic information about your candidate clients, your next step is to do some first-hand research about them and/or what they do. This step can be time intensive, but the extra effort can really pay off and be a lot of fun besides.

If you want to sell to retailers, go shopping at their stores. Take note of the stock, the atmosphere, the lighting, the merchandising, the background music and/or fragrance and the store layout, as if you were a potential customer. Well, you are one, aren't you?

Monitor the service: is there adequate sales help or is anyone helping you at all? Does a salesperson come up to you or do you have to find one? If someone does help you, do they inquire about your need for their products and try to help, or do they stand behind the counter and ask, *"Did you find what you wanted?"* Do they seem to care what you say?

Most importantly, notice how you feel during your shopping experience from the minute you walk in the store to the minute you leave. Would you shop there again? Why? Why not? You can't get that kind of information sitting at home in front of a computer or by reading a catalog or industry statistics.

If you want to sell to restaurants, develop a working knowledge of their menus, be aware of the professionalism and proficiency of the wait staff and notice if a manager comes by to see how everything tasted. Compare one restaurant to others in terms of their décor, the cleanliness of the bathrooms and the whole dining experience each provides. Eat up and enjoy; if you're going to be selling to those restaurants, you should expect to be doing a whole lot of eating there.

Gaining research about an industry you don't know anything about is really easy to do because chances are that you already know someone who can provide you with information and insight about their industry. For example, let's say you're marketing to accountants but you don't know anything about the accounting business.

If you have or know an accountant, take that person to lunch and pick their brain, focusing the conversation on the problem that your product or service can solve without trying to sell them, and listen to their honest feedback. Even though this is not a sales call, chances are that your accountant friend will be very interested in what you're offering, and if he's not, he'll happily refer you to other accountants he knows who might be.

If you don't have or know an accountant, you'll find plenty in your local Chamber of Commerce or Google "accountant association" and the name of your city. The organization will have an online member directory, and all you have to do is pick up the phone.

Making the Call

You may be leery about calling because you're afraid Mr. Bigg will say *"no"* and you'll be embarrassed, or you just don't know what to say. No wonder. The Traditional System's advice about how to make cold phone calls is daunting and falls into three categories:

- *The Prod*: Getting past the gatekeeper is considered a major challenge. How can you sell yourself to Mr. Bigg if his secretary won't put you through or you keep getting voice mail?

- *The Pitch*: You don't have much time before Mr. Bigg hangs up, so you need to get it all out as fast as possible

- *The Push*: Once you're on the phone with Mr. Bigg, you're determined to get that meeting, no matter how much he resists

The Prod

This is it; you're going to call Mr. Bigg from out of the blue. You gather up all of your courage, take a deep breath and punch the number, determined to speak to Mr. Bigg.

Susan: *"John Bigg's office, this is Susan."*

Uh, oh, it's the secretary. You've got to get past her to get a shot at Mr. Bigg.

> You: *"Is Mr. Bigg in?"*
> Susan: *"He's in a meeting. Who's calling?"*
> You: *"I'm Steve Thomas, and I want to talk to Mr. Bigg about his accounting needs."* (You launch into your 30-second commercial.)
> Susan (interrupting): *"We already have an accountant. Thanks for calling. Goodbye."*

If your cold calls go like this, you probably believe the secretary is there to act as a buffer between her boss and the rest of the world. I spent five years as a secretary and I can tell you that rather than being an obstacle, the secretary can be your biggest ally–if you treat her right.

The Secretary's Secret

If you've never been a clerical worker, you should know that for the most part, the job stinks. Essentially, you are invisible unless someone wants something, and you are thought of as little more than a pair of hands with a brain attached, one that you are not expected to use much.

Your opinion is not sought and does not count. People who are right in front of you talk around you as if you do not exist, and your only authority is to order lunch or office supplies. You are not expected to read or care about what you are typing or filing, are easily replaced by a temporary worker, and people are shocked if you express any kind of ambition.

That said, many secretaries and administrative assistants take great pride in their work, especially if they work with senior executives at large companies. But for the majority of clerical workers, especially those who yearn not to be one, it's a secure but degrading job. If you can type fast and accurately enough and are proficient in the latest software, you can always get work to pay your bills and get your ego soothed elsewhere.

Knowing this, your best tactic is to treat the secretary as an intelligent human being, rather than as an obstacle to circumvent. You want her on your side because she can be your biggest help or worst hindrance.

There is one sure-fire way to make the secretary your ally from your very first call: just use her name and then ask her a favor.

Susan: *"John Bigg's office, this is Susan."*
You: *"Susan, I wonder if you can help me. My name is Steve Thomas, and I mailed John some information last week about how recent upgrades in mobile technology may impact your company. Do you know if he got it?"*

When you treat the secretary with respect and dignity, she will give you all kinds of useful information:

- Susan is a temp or is filling in for John's secretary, so she doesn't see his mail
- Susan is John's secretary, but she does not screen his mail
- Susan says John has been on vacation, out sick, out of town, preparing for a big meeting, etc. Your material is still on his desk, unopened
- Susan says John got your material and said you should talk to Mary Small, the Vice President of Operations, and she'll transfer you
- Susan says John wants to see you. Can you come in next week?

When you tell Susan what your call is about right up front, you treat her like a professional who should know what you're talking about. Chances are excellent that she won't, so she'll either put you through to Mr. Bigg or someone else. Remember, if Mr. Bigg is going to be your client, you're going to be working with Susan, so having a good relationship with her from the outset is essential.

The Pitch

According to the Traditional System, you only have 10 or 15 seconds before the line goes dead, so you need to break out your best elevator speech:

> "My name is Thomas Smith, and I work for Sun Solutions, the leading provider of inventory management software. Our Track Connect product has won awards for technology advancement and provides full supply chain management capabilities. We have been in business for 30 years and have offices in 60 countries."

> "Hi, this is Laura Schneider, CEO/President of ZealSpin, Inc., an interactive marketing company that shows companies how to integrate their offline and online marketing."

> "My name is Chris Winston. I help HR departments keep track of employees, salaries and benefits. If your current system isn't keeping up with your needs, I can fix inaccurate reports, install software upgrades, help you meet regulatory requirements and make the system easier to use. Since I specialize in HR systems, I understand all of your unique needs, and stay current on what's essential for you to know."

> "I'm Dr. Virginia Lee. I guide my clients to optimal health and relief from pain. As a chiropractor, I provide hands-on healing to help you relieve pain, feel better, and get more out of life. I treat back and neck pain, headaches, disc injuries, carpal tunnel, and much more. I have helped hundreds of people live pain free, with increased flexibility and improved health."

The whole idea of an elevator speech is to impress the person you're talking to. Unfortunately, it almost always creates the wrong impression.

Elevator speeches are blatant sales pitches, and instead of interesting Mr. Bigg, you're really alienating him.

Webster's definitions of "pitch" includes, *"...to throw, usually with a particular objective or toward a particular point; to sell or advertise, especially in a high pressure way; to utter glibly and insincerely."*

So, when you use an elevator speech to begin your First Contact phone call, you are glibly and insincerely using high-pressure sales tactics to throw yourself at Mr. Bigg. You're talking *at* him, not *to* him and certainly not having a conversation *with* him. Is this the first impression you really want to make?

The Push

According to the Traditional System, the goal of a phone sales call is not to sell your product, but to get an appointment so you can do an in-person presentation. I couldn't disagree more. The real purpose of a First Contact phone call to is to establish the basis for a working relationship between you and Mr. Bigg.

Once Mr. Bigg feels at ease with you on the phone, he will be receptive to your suggestions and want to move to the next step, either a face-to-face meeting or a continuance of your conversation at a later time. If he's not, your chances of making a sale are practically zero.

Going Beyond "Hello"

Be prepared to speak to Mr. Bigg when you call him, especially if he's a small business owner. In large companies, secretaries are so scarce these days that most people in authority answer their own phones, and besides, a lot of executives don't want anyone screening their calls for them.

Although the Traditional System will have you believe you only have a few seconds before Mr. Bigg hangs up, in reality, he will give you all the time in the world if your call is about him, his company, family and/or situation and not yourself or your company.

This the structure of a Contrarian System First Contact phone call:

- Introduce yourself/Why you're calling
- Discuss his situation
- Suggest you can help
- Determine the next step
- Follow-up

Introduce Yourself/Why You're Calling

The very first thing you say and the way you say it will be Mr. Bigg's first and lasting impression of you, so you want to have your introduction down pat.

Keep your introduction short, simple, to the point and most importantly, make it about him, not you.

- Make a referral: *"John Jones at ABC Corporation suggested I contact you"*
- Recap a function you both attended: *"It was a pleasure meeting you last week at the meeting of ..."*

- Summarize his comments: *"I heard you speak last week and I was intrigued by your new approach to ..."* or *"I read your article in the latest issue of ..."*

Use these openings if you have them, but chances are that you will have none of them. Instead, make a general comment about an industry trend, news about Mr. Bigg's company or himself, the company's latest venture, a change you've noticed in their packaging, an event he or the company is, was or will be involved with–something, anything Mr. Bigg can relate to.

If you do your homework about Mr. Bigg and/or his company, the products and/or services he provides, how his company stacks up against his colleagues in his industry, what he is involved with and what is happening in the world affecting him, his family or company, you can easily find plenty to talk about.

Discuss His Situation

Now suggest – not tell – Mr. Bigg he may be faced with a problem or better yet, an opportunity, and then briefly discuss this problem or opportunity without offering solutions. Contrary to what the Traditional System teaches, one of the worst things you can do is to offer Mr. Bigg solutions as an incentive for him to want to meet you.

If you offer solutions, claim to be the answer to Mr. Bigg's problem, or give examples of how you solved similar problems for other people or companies, Mr. Bigg will know you are trying to sell him, and you will destroy any credibility he has given you up to this point.

But when you discuss an issue Mr. Bigg may be facing without offering solutions, he will automatically credit you with having insight into his situation and assume you have some ideas on how to help him, which will make him want to know you better.

Suggest You Can Help

By this time, Mr. Bigg is feeling good about you, and he naturally wants to know something about you. Only now do you briefly mention what you do and how there's a possibility you might be able to help him, such as, "*If you have a few minutes, I can walk you through our website. The address is www....*"

If you want Mr. Bigg to want to know more about you, say as little as possible about yourself, your company and what you're selling, downplay your own importance and keep your conversation focused on him, his family or company and his situation.

Determine the Next Step

You've gotten Mr. Bigg interested and perhaps intrigued; now it's time to determine with him the next logical step, such as arranging a meeting, exchanging emails, sending a catalogue, placing an order, walking him through filling out the paperwork, etc.

Rather than a teeth-pulling ordeal, moving to the next step should come effortlessly and automatically. In fact, don't be surprised if Mr. Bigg takes the lead here and moves himself to the next step by volunteering information or scheduling the meeting with you.

Following Up

You've had a great phone call with Mr. Bigg, created the basis for a possible relationship and moved to the next step. Since you initiated this call, you must assume total responsibility for following up with Mr. Bigg and eventually making the sale.

Use your CRM to not only schedule your upcoming meeting with Mr. Bigg in your calendar, but send an invitation that, depending upon the email/CRM system he uses, will put the meeting on his calendar as well. You'll then need to confirm the meeting with Mr. Bigg by phone shortly before you meet.

When you take responsibility for follow-up, it proves you are capable, reliable, can take the initiative, see a project through and get things done–everything Mr. Bigg expects from someone he does business with.

Traditional vs. Contrarian System Phone Calls

You have a consulting service for families who have children with autism spectrum disorders, and you want to partner with companies serving those families. You've identified a manufacturer of special educational toys, books and teaching materials and have the CEO on the phone, so you launch into your elevator speech:

John (answering his phone): *"John Bigg."*
You: *"Mr. Bigg, my name is Stephanie Murphy, and I run a consulting service for families with autistic children. I'm calling to see if there is a way we can work together to increase your sales.*

"As a former special education teacher with 20 years' experience, I have an unparalleled insight into the unique needs of these families. I believe I could help your company enormously. When can we meet?"

According to the Traditional System, your elevator speech, combined with a strong pitch for a meeting, is supposed to wow Mr. Bigg into wanting to see you. Unfortunately, it usually doesn't:

John: *"That may be true, but right now we're full up with consultants. Email me some information and let's keep in touch. Thanks for calling."*

If you use the Traditional System approach to First Contact cold calls, you can expect to be off the phone with Mr. Bigg within a few minutes and never know why he cut you off. But if you make a Contrarian System First Contact call that is all about Mr. Bigg instead of yourself, you'll get a completely different outcome:

John: *"John Bigg."*
You: *"Mr. Bigg, my name is Stephanie Murphy of Therapy Marketing Services, and I read in Special Families Magazine that your firm is launching a new line of therapeutic toys for autistic children this year."*
John: *"Yes, we are."*
You: *"From the information I read, I gather you are going to market these toys directly to parents, but I wonder if you had considered marketing these toys to special needs therapists and educators as well. Are you familiar with play therapy?"*
John: *"Yes, of course."*
You: *"Then you know the key to a successful program is matching the right toys with the child's needs. Much of the time, a therapist can readily design an effective program with out-of-the-box toys.*

"But autistic children are often non-communicative, may have difficulty socializing with others and are extremely sensitive to light, sound and touch. Regular toys just won't suffice for these children.

"That's why I wanted to talk with you about your new therapeutic toys. They are desperately needed, and it occurred to me I might be able to help you get your products to the teachers, therapists and families you want to reach in the most cost-effective way."
John: *"How would you do that?"*

> You: *"Part of our program involves arranging demonstrations with school districts and in-services with hospitals and clinics. Your products are so unique and I know many specialists who would want to evaluate their effectiveness with their students and patients."*
>
> John: *"Perhaps you* can *help us. We've been in the toy business a long time, but we've never done anything like this before. We sure could use someone with your insight. Can you come in next week to talk to us?"*

JACKPOT! Mr. Bigg has convinced himself you can help him and is eager to see you. And you did all this without using a manipulative sales pitch, being the least bit nervous or even having him go to your website.

The key to a successful First Contact phone call is to remember that this call is not about you; it's about Mr. Bigg. The instant it becomes about you, Mr. Bigg will know he's being hustled, cut the phone call short and cut you out of his life.

Voice Mail

But sometimes you can't reach Mr. Bigg and all you get is voice mail:

"This is John Bigg. I'm not in, so leave a message and I'll call you back."

So you leave a message:

"Mr. Bigg, this is Robin Sloan of Better Budgeting. (You go into your elevator speech). I believe I can help your company achieve its goals. Please call me at 222-555-1212."

A week goes by and he doesn't call, so you try it again:

"Mr. Bigg, this is Robin Sloan of Better Budgeting again. I left you a message last week about how I can help your company, and have emailed you information. Please let me know if you have any questions about it. My number is 222-555-1212. Thank you."

You let another week go by, and with gritted teeth and a sinking feeling, you try it one last time:

"Mr. Bigg, this is Robin Sloan of Better Budgeting again. I know you must be very busy not to return phone calls. I just want five minutes of your time to discuss how we can help your company. My number is 222-555-1212. Thank you."

You never hear from Mr. Bigg or anyone at that company, and with a sigh, you delete him from your database. Why didn't he call you back? It could be any number of reasons:

- He's out sick, on vacation or a business trip, is getting ready to go on vacation or a business trip, or has left the company and forgot to change his voice mail
- He's working on a major project or is putting out fires, and everything else is lost in the shuffle
- He's not the most organized person; his desk is a giant mess and your messages are probably in there somewhere
- He's a solopreneur with a bootstrap startup and won't need an accountant for several years, assuming he stays in business that long
- He has a long-standing relationship with someone who crunches his numbers and he hopes that if he ignores you, you'll get the message intuitively and stop bothering him, which you eventually do

Leave one follow-up voice mail with Mr. Bigg, and call back one week later. If you're still getting voice mail, don't leave another message, don't take it personally and don't assume this means anything.

If you're calling a large company, hit "0"–chances are you will get a live person. If the phone system is so convoluted you can't get a live person, hit an extension for a department that will answer, like sales or accounting, and ask whoever answers how to reach Mr. Bigg.

Once in a while, you will encounter a company where there is no live operator and no one answers the phone or returns messages. If this happens, ask yourself if you want to do business with a company that makes it so difficult to contact them. After all, if you can't get through, neither can their customers–that is, if they have any left.

Conversely, voice mail may be the only way to reach someone who is intensely busy, out of their office or travels a lot. Fortunately, most people on the road check their voice mail daily and will get their emails on their cell phone.

But because of their schedules or other matters that have nothing to do with you, even though they are getting your messages, they may not be able to call you back any time soon, so don't take delays personally. Also remember that you are not a priority to them right now.

There is a very fine line between staying in touch and being a pest. Leave a maximum of two voice mails over three weeks, and if you're still not getting a response, let this one go for now. You have no way of knowing what's going on in Mr. Bigg's life or company, so give it a rest and call back in a month or so.

But if you've reached Mr. Bigg or his secretary and been told to call back, when should you call again? Don't guess or offer a time; just ask: *"When would you suggest I get back in touch with you?"* and they will tell you.

Chapter Eight
FIRST CONTACT: BY EMAIL/LETTER

As often happens with busy people, you might not be able to get Mr. Bigg on the phone, so you decide to make First Contact by email. Sure, it's easy (if you know his email address), fast and cheap, but making First Contact by email has tremendous pitfalls.

It's a good bet that you delete junk emails and won't open emails with attachments from people you don't know. Well, like it or not, Mr. Bigg does exactly the same thing, and that's assuming your email even makes it to his in-box; thanks to spam filters, he may never even see it.

The best way to use email is after you have spoken to Mr. Bigg. The second best way is to leave a message for Mr. Bigg telling him why you're calling and that you're sending him information about it. This way, he'll be expecting your email, will open it and read it.

Don't think you can trick Mr. Bigg into opening your email by using a snazzy subject line. This gimmick may work once, but you'll come across as amateurish and insincere, and destroy any chance you might have had of getting in the door or making your sale.

On the other hand, if you really want to catch Mr. Bigg's attention, send him a real snail mail letter–the kind with an envelope and stamp. When email first hit the business world, it was new, exciting and cutting-edge. But now that email is commonplace, regular mail will stand out as unusual, simply because a letter exists in the physical world.

Mr. Bigg has to hold your letter while he's reading it and then do something with it: file it, put it on a pile, give it to someone else or throw it out. But it just may float on his desk, something that can't happen with your email unless he prints it out, which is unlikely.

Whether you hit send or stuff envelopes, using the mail to make First Contact has pros and cons:

E-mail/Letter First Contact Pros

- Mail is a relatively inexpensive form of advertising/marketing compared to other mediums
- You have complete control over what your message says and who it reaches
- Mail can be very effective for reaching consumers, especially when you are using couponing, sampling or a limited-time sale to generate sales
- Mail can be very effective to begin a conversation or follow-up with potential business clients
- With the right type of persuasive writing, you can sell virtually anything to anyone
- You can easily track the success of your mailing campaigns

E-mail/Letter First Contact Cons

- Response rates can range from less than 1% to up to 10%. Like all forms of advertising, half of your budget will be wasted; you just won't know which half
- Direct mail is usually considered junk mail and typically tossed without being opened
- Unwanted emails from strangers are usually deleted without being opened, assuming they make it through spam filters
- Since repetition is essential in marketing, mailings must be done consistently over a long period of time for maximum effectiveness

- It may be challenging or expensive to obtain accurate mailing lists
- In order to comply with federal law, you must obtain a person's approval before you put them on your email list or you may be branded a spammer and subject to fines and other penalties
- Mail is passive–all you can do is reach out and hope someone eventually responds

All that said, when combined with a mix of offline and online marketing strategies, and when it's done consistently over a long period of time and targeted to your specific clientele, email/snail mail can be an extremely cost-effective way to build your business.

Traditional System Mailings	**Contrarian System Mailings**
Short term, sales-oriented	Long term, relationship-oriented
"Splash" approach–sporadic marketing	"Drip" approach–continuous marketing
Shotgun approach–hope to hit them	Rifle approach–good chance of hitting them
Upfront costs can be large	Upfront costs can be nominal
Can take 12–24 months to recoup costs	Can take weeks to recoup costs
Making a sale is an isolated event	Making a sale is an on-going process
Requires a large, often rented, database	Requires you to build your own contact list
Best when combined with other forms of marketing	Can be very effective all by itself

Traditional System Mailings	Contrarian System Mailings
Often involves printers, writers, mailers	Can be done by one person at a computer
Appeal to negative emotions: fear, greed	Appeal to positive emotions: joy, prosperity
"Slippery slope" pressures buyers	No pressure, buyers are intrigued
Often uses a headline that screams "ad"	Composed as a regular letter
Contains a sense of urgency	Contains a sense of possibilities
Uses hard sell pitching and hustling	Uses soft sell explaining and persuading
Market tends to be broad/little research	Market is very narrow/research is critical
Premiums/incentives are essential	Premiums/incentives are incidental
Text assumes people can be manipulated	Text assumes people can make decisions
Text is written for mass audience	Text is customized for individuals
The use of templates is obvious	The use of templates is undetectable
Text speaks *at* buyer; demands action	Text speaks *to* buyer; invites opportunity
Text tells the whole story	Text serves as an introduction
Buyer is responsible for next step	Seller is responsible for next step
Focus is on the quantity of mailings	Focus is on the quality of relationships
Are all about what the seller wants to sell	Are all about what the buyer may want/need

Traditional System Mailings	Contrarian System Mailings
Seller has the solution to buyer's problem	Seller may have a solution to buyer's problem
Repeat sales require starting all over	Repeat sales flow naturally
The buyer is "them out there"	The buyer is "me in here"

How Not to Write a Sales Letter

You've probably received at least one email or sales letter like this one that was sent to me:

> *Many businesses have discovered that in-house collections–staff telephone calls, invoicing, collections letters–are costing them more than the effort is worth. In fact, they find their collection department actually loses money. Our professional collection agency can handle every detail of your collections and recover more money at a lower cost.*
>
> *Collections are our business. During our 20 years in the collection business, we have refined a successful system that produces exceptional results. What's more, there is no fee for this service. We only take a percentage of what we collect. If we don't collect, we aren't paid!*
>
> *Please review the list of companies that use our service. Call them and ask them about our efficiency. Their satisfaction is a better endorsement than we could ever give.*
>
> *We have a special introductory offer for you. Try us out for three months at half our regular percentage rate. To receive this special price, you must mail in the enclosed card within two weeks. After October 31, this special offer will no longer be available. Call us today. We look forward to helping you collect more of the money that is owed you.*

Or maybe something like this one:

How to Save 75%–80% on Office Systems Furniture

Atlas Office Interiors wants to help your business save up to 80% on office systems furniture. We specialize in refurbished and pre-owned name-brand workstations including Haworth, Herman Miller and Steelcase. Why pay full price for new workstations when you can get beautiful, professional-quality pre-owned and refurbished systems furniture at up to 80% off?

As a full service dealer, we have products and services to help you design, furnish and install workstations, reception areas and conference rooms. We are networked with wholesalers and distributors throughout the U.S. to offer you an extensive range of products to meet all of your needs and at a price that is guaranteed to fit your budget. And, we will personally deliver and install your office furniture for you so your project is done correctly, on-time and on-budget.

For a free quote, please call us today at 1-800-777-7777 or visit us online at www.officefurnituresales.com. Our website has many pictures of the furniture we have in stock and our current specials. If you want an amazing deal, check out our website.

If you have office furniture you want to sell, we would love the opportunity to bid on it. We work with brokers and dealers throughout the United States and Canada who will offer you top dollar for your used office furniture. For more information, please call us at 1-800-777-7777.

Ditch the Pitch

The idea behind these kinds of sales letters is to intrigue, entice and engage you as a potential client and motivate you to take action, such as picking up the phone, going to their website, returning the postcard, etc., to indicate you're interested in purchasing whatever they're selling.

Think for a minute how you respond to such blatant sales letters. Are you intrigued, enticed and engaged, or are you turned off, bored and disgusted? If you're sending out these kind of letters–whether by email or snail mail–STOP! You're wasting your time and money, and far from attracting new clients, you're actually repelling them.

According to Direct Marketing News, a leading industry trade journal, the average response rate for direct mail in 2012 was just 4.4% and a mere 0.12% for email. Putting it simply, for every $100 you spend on direct mail, you can expect to make $4.40 by using letters and only 12 cents using email. Does this make sense?

Actually it might, if you're a large corporation or marketing/PR agency and it's not your money you're spending, if you're selling in a wide geographic area, don't need to or care about having relationships with your potential clients and/or are only focused on one-shot product sales, like magazine subscriptions.

But if you're selling locally, do business face-to-face, want your clients to do business with you over and over and refer their friends and colleagues to you, pitching and hustling simply doesn't work.

The next time you get some junk mail or spam email, notice how the writers tell you about themselves or what they want you to buy, and especially notice how you feel about them as they do so. Well, that's just how Mr. Bigg feels about you when you write a Traditional System sales letter that's all about you.

Traditional System Sales Letters

The reason Traditional System cold call sales letters have such a low success rate is because they use key psychological triggers to manipulate your thinking and subtly pressure you to make a purchase–none of which you're supposed to notice. Traditional System sales letters typically have these basic components:

- Get your attention
- Why they're writing

- What they're selling
- Why you should buy it now
- What else you'll get if you buy what they're selling right now
- What you should do next
- What else you need to know to motivate you to take action immediately

Let's look at the structure of a typical Traditional System sales letter in more detail:[5]

Get Their Attention

Assuming the reader has opened your email or envelope, the next step is to get their attention. The opening headline is the first thing that your reader will look at. If it doesn't catch their attention, you can kiss your letter goodbye.

People have a very short attention span and usually sort their mail over the wastebasket. If the headline doesn't call out to them and pique their interest, they will just stop and throw your letter away. The following are three headline-generating templates that are proven to get attention.

"HOW TO _____"

People love to know how to do things. When combined with a powerful benefit, the "How to" headline always gets people's attention. In fact, they're probably the two most powerful words you can use in a headline.

"SECRETS OF _____ REVEALED!"

People always want to know insider secrets. We love to know things that other people aren't privy to. Knowledge is power and those who have it feel powerful. Besides that, most of us enjoy a good mystery, especially in the end when the "secret" is revealed.

*"WARNING: DON'T EVEN THINK OF _____
UNTIL YOU _____ "*

People are motivated by fear of loss more than the promise of gain and the "warning" headline screams fear. The word "warning" demands attention, and combined with something of interest to the reader, is a very powerful headline.

Identify the Problem

Now that you have your reader's attention, you need to gain their interest by spelling out their problem and how it feels to have that problem. The reader should say to himself, "Yeah, that's exactly how I feel" when they read your copy. In fact, you shouldn't stop there. Pretend that it's an open wound that you're rubbing salt into.

This technique is called, "problem–agitate." You present the problem, then agitate it so that they really feel the pain and agony of their situation. People are such strong creatures of habit that we rarely change our ways unless we feel great amounts of pain. In fact, companies are no different.

Most people trudge along doing the same old thing until things get so bad that they have to make a change. For example, if you were selling garage door openers, you might agitate the problem by telling a short story about what happens when it doesn't work, such as:

> *"There's nothing worse than getting home in the evening and not having your garage door open. It's dark outside and after tripping on the porch step you search for your front door key.*
>
> *"Finally, you find it only to scratch your new front door up trying to find the keyhole. Exhausted, you get inside and plop down on the couch just when you remember your car is still running in your driveway."*

In this scenario, the problem was a faulty garage door opener and the agitation is all the terrible things that happen because of the faulty garage door opener.

Provide the Solution

Now that you've built your reader's interest by making them feel the pain, it's time to provide the solution. This is the part of the sales letter where you boldly stake your claim that you can solve the reader's problem.

In this section, you will introduce yourself, your product and/or your service. Relieve the reader's mind by telling them that there's no need to struggle through all their problems because your product or service will solve it for them.

Present Your Credentials

In most cases, after you have introduced yourself and your product or service, your reader is thinking, "Yeah, sure, he can fix my problem. That's what they all say." So now it's important to hit them right away with the reason why you can be trusted. List your credentials, including any one of the following:

- *Successful case studies*
- *Prestigious companies (or people) you have done business with*
- *The length of time you've been in your field of expertise*
- *Conferences where you have spoken*
- *Important awards or recognitions*

Your reader should get the impression after reading this section that "you've been there and done that" with great success and that they can expect the same results.

Show the Benefits

Now it's time to tell the reader how they will personally benefit from your product or service. Don't make the common mistake of telling all about the features of your product without talking about the benefits. People are interested, not so much in you or even your product or service, but what it will do for them.

Get a piece of paper and draw a line down the center of the paper. Now write all the features of your product or service on the left. Think about the obvious benefits and not-so-obvious benefits of the each feature and write them down on the right side of the paper. Most of the time, your product will have hidden benefits that people won't naturally think of.

For example, a hot tub not only soothes and relaxes your muscles, but it also gives you an opportunity to talk to your spouse without interruptions. The hidden benefit is greater communication with your spouse and ultimately a better marriage!

Bullet point each benefit to make it easier to read. Think about every possible benefit your reader may derive from your product or service. In many cases, people will buy a product or service based on only one of the benefits you list.

Give Social Proof

After you've presented all your benefits, the reader will again begin to doubt you, even though they secretly want all your claimed benefits to be true. To build your credibility and believability, present your reader with testimonials from satisfied customers.

Testimonials are powerful selling tools that prove your claims to be true. To make your testimonials even more powerful, include pictures of your customers with their names and addresses (at least the city and state).

You might even ask if you can use their phone number. Most readers won't call, but it is a powerful statement to include their complete contact information. It demonstrates that you are real and so are the testimonials.

Make Your Offer

Your offer is the most important part of your sales letter. A great offer can overcome mediocre copy, but great copy cannot overcome a mediocre offer. Your offer should be irresistible. You want your reader to say to themselves, "I'd be stupid not to take advantage of this deal."

Your offer can come in many different formats. The best offers are usually an attractive combination of price, terms and free gifts. For example, if you were selling a car, your offer might be a discounted retail price, low interest rate and a free year of gas.

When developing your offer, you should always try to raise its value by adding on products or services, rather than by lowering your price. Include vivid explanations of the benefits of the additional products or services you are offering in order to raise the perceived value of your offer.

Give a Guarantee

To make your offer even more irresistible, you need to take all the risk out of the purchase. Remember that people have a built-in fear that they are going to get ripped off. How many times have you purchased a product and got stuck with it because the merchant wouldn't give your money back?

Give the absolute strongest guarantee you are able to give. If you aren't confident enough in your product or service to give a strong guarantee, you should think twice about offering it to the public.

In reality, almost all small businesses already have a very strong guarantee, but don't realize it. If you had an irate customer that wanted their money back, would you just say, "No, I'm sorry, I will not give your money back?" Probably not. If they insist on getting their money back, in most cases you'll give it back to them.

Most businesses already have a strong guarantee, but don't hold it up and trumpet it for fear that a lot of people would take them up on it. That simply doesn't happen. When was the last time you asked for a full refund on something? Probably not for a while.

Inject Scarcity

Most people take their time responding to offers, even when they are irresistible. There are many reasons why people procrastinate on investing in a solution, including:

- They don't feel enough pain to make a change
- They are too busy and just forget
- They don't feel that the perceived value outweighs your asking price
- They are just plain lazy

To motivate people to take action, they usually need an extra incentive. Remember that people are more motivated to act by the fear of loss rather than gain. That's exactly what you are doing when you inject scarcity into your letter.

When people think there is a scarce supply of something they need, they usually rush to get some of it. You can create a feeling of scarcity by telling your reader that either the quantity is in limited supply or that your offer is valid for only a limited time period. Your offer could sound something like this: "If you purchase by (future date) you will get the entire set of free bonuses."

One word of caution: if you make an offer, you need to live up to it. If you go back on your word after the deadline date, you will begin to erode the trust and confidence your customers have come to expect from you.

Call to Action

Do not assume that your reader knows what to do to receive the benefits from your offer. You must spell out how to make the order in very clear and concise language. Whether it's picking up the phone and making the call, filling out an order form, emailing or faxing the order form to your office, you must tell them exactly how to order from you.

Your call to action must be action-oriented. You can do this using words like "Pick up the phone and call now!" or "Tear off the order form and send it in today!" or "Come to our store by Friday." Be explicit and succinct in your instructions.

Plant your call to action throughout your letter. If you are asking the reader to call your free information line, perhaps some of the testimonials might say, "When I called their free information line ..."

Your offer might say, "When you call our free information line ..." then when you give the call to action at the end of the letter, people won't be surprised or confused. It will be consistent with what you said all throughout your letter.

Give a Warning

A good sales letter will continue to build emotion right up to the very end. In fact, your letter should continue to build emotion even after your call to action. Using the "risk of loss" strategy, tell the reader what would happen if they didn't take advantage of your offer. Perhaps they would continue to:

- *Struggle day to day to make ends meet*
- *Work too hard just to get a few customers*
- *Lose the opportunity to receive all your valuable bonuses*
- *Keep getting what they've always got*
- *Watch other companies get all the business*

Try to paint a graphic picture in the mind of the reader about the consequences of not taking action now. Remind them just how terrible their current state is and that it just doesn't have to be that way.

Close with a Reminder

Always include a postscript (P.S.). Believe it or not, your P.S. is the third most read element of your sales letter. In your postscript, you want to remind them of your irresistible offer. If you've used scarcity in your sales letter, include your call to action and then remind them of the limited time or quantity offer. It sounds like a simple step, but postscripts get noticed.

Perhaps in some cases, Traditional System sales letters could work if you're selling to some consumers who typically fall for these manipulative tactics and respond to artificially-induced triggers of pain, fear and lack. But when it comes to selling to other businesses or sophisticated buyers, this approach will backfire against you big time.

Contrarian System Sales Letters

This is because when you're selling to businesses, you're dealing with Mr. Bigg-the boss, the one who has the authority to say yes. He got to be the boss by starting, buying and/or building his company, and because he's an intelligent, highly-trained professional, he typically makes purchasing decisions for himself, his family and his business based on logic, not feelings.

And assuming Mr. Bigg is a consumer, having the same kind of respect for his intelligence you would want him to have for yours is essential. He may, in fact, need, want or be interested in what you're selling, but the approach you take with him and the language you use to connect with him will determine if he buys from you or someone else or at all.

> *The key to writing a Contrarian System sales letter is to write to Mr. Bigg about what is important to him, not what is important to you. You will know what's important to him from all that the research you did about him and his company.*

This is the key difference between the "shallow and broad" approach of marketing and the "narrow and deep" approach to selling – instead of reaching large numbers of potential clients with a general message hoping they'll respond, you're reaching out to a limited number of people on an individual basis and starting a conversation (albeit in writing) with them.

While the Traditional System uses overt, hard-pressure sales tactics and presumes people will fall for them, the Contrarian System uses a soft sell approach that combines common sense, sound business judgment and an understanding of basic human psychology, along with an inherent respect for the people you're reaching.

The structure of a Contrarian System sales letter is exactly the same as a First Contact phone call except it's in writing:

- First to second paragraph: Introduction/why you're writing
- Second to third paragraph: Discuss Mr. Bigg's situation
- Third to fourth paragraph: Suggest you can help
- Fourth to fifth paragraph: What you will do next

Introduction/Why You're Writing

Your opening line or paragraph should be written to catch Mr. Bigg's attention, draw him into the body of the letter and make him want to keep reading. Just like your First Contact phone call, start your letter with something that involves Mr. Bigg personally or professionally or affects him, his company or his family. This will automatically draw him into the body of your letter and make him want to keep reading.

Discuss Mr. Bigg's Situation

Again, just like your phone call, suggest – not tell – Mr. Bigg he may be faced with a problem or better yet, an area of opportunity, and then briefly discuss this problem or area of opportunity without offering solutions.

When you discuss an issue Mr. Bigg may be facing without offering solutions, he will assume you can help him, which will make him interested in knowing more about what you have to offer. Unlike the Traditional System, you will not be manipulating Mr. Bigg into making a sale; his desire to buy from you will come from within himself.

Suggest You Can Help

By this time, Mr. Bigg is feeling very good about you, and he naturally wants to know something about your company and what it can do for him. Only now do you briefly mention who you are and how there's a possibility you might be able to help him.

This should intentionally be written as an aside with the tone of, *"Oh, by the way, here's some information on me, but it's really not too important."*

Be sure to write as little as possible about yourself, your company and your product or service, and keep your letter focused on him, his company and his situation.

What You Will Do Next

Most Traditional System sales letters end limply, implying that you are no longer responsible for making the sale and it's all up to Mr. Bigg now:

"I look forward to hearing from you"

"Please let me know if you are interested"

"There's no cost. No obligation. Just go to the website to sign up"

"Act today! You don't want to miss this special discount"

When you use these phrases, you may think you're being polite, but you really come across as being weak, passive, and wimpy or pushy, aggressive and helpless.

The best way to end your letter is to cordially tell Mr. Bigg you will be calling him in a week and then thank him for his time. After all, if everything goes right, you're going to be taking up a great deal more of it very soon.

Chapter Nine
SALES LETTERS MAKEOVERS

Here is a very easy way to know if you have written an effective sales letter and what to do about it if you haven't:

- Count the number of I's: I, me, my, us, our, and/or we referring to yourself, your company or your products or services
- Count the number of You's: you, your, Mr. Bigg's name, the name of his company and/or other people you know or have talked to in his company
- The use of we, us and our when referring to yourself and Mr. Bigg cancel each other out and are not counted
- If there are more I's than you's, or if your letter is clearly about you even if it has more you's than I's, delete it or rip it up and start all over. You've written about the wrong person

Here are some real Traditional System First Contact sales letters, followed by a Contrarian System makeover of the same letter (the names have been changed, but the formatting is exactly the same as in the original text). At the bottom of each letter is its "I versus You" score.

Whittaker Home Comfort Company – Traditional System

Dear Homeowner,
With winter just around the corner, the Whittaker Home Comfort Company launches its 60th year of service to our city. Over the years, we have become a respected fixture in the community, building our reputation one satisfied customer at a time.

The Whittaker organization has always provided only the highest quality heating and cooling equipment, such as Lennox and Trane, prompt, 24-hour service by factory-trained technicians, concern for your family's comfort and budget and just plain, old-fashioned value in all of our dealings.

To offer you the most affordable heating and air conditioning systems possible, we feature a variety of money-saving specials during the year like equipment discounts, add-ons, special 0% financing, trade-ins, rebates and so forth.

Our special for this season offers you a great opportunity – a generous $1,075 cash rebate when you purchase an Xii system. And to make the deal even sweeter, 0% financing for six months or a FREE 10-year parts and labor warranty at no extra charge – a $450 value! There are no gimmicks, no hidden costs. Just buy now and you have a truly outstanding bargain. Don't forget to ask us about Utility Rebates for added savings.

*Whittaker offers a variety of other perks and benefits as well. Take for example our **free in-home Comfort Evaluations and Estimates.** They cost you nothing and are essential in providing the optimum system for your needs. This will grow increasingly important with the upward spiral of gas and electricity costs.*

*Likewise, our **Second Opinion Service** is a valuable tool. If you are indecisive about another company's offer, we will look over the deal with an expert eye and give you our opinion. Again, there is no cost. We offer special financial plans and specialized equipment to make your home healthier and more energy efficient. **Planned Service ... periodic maintenance plans ... duct cleaning ... even attic insulation.** This list seems endless!*

*Simply put, we feel that the biggest advantage in selecting Whittaker is the long tradition of caring service – before, during and for years after the sale. **We have a solution for any home comfort problem. Give us a call today and let's talk.***

Sincerely yours,
Joe Whittaker

P.S.: Whittaker Home Comfort Company is working hard to keep our air clean. Ask about our ozone friendly cooling equipment and help us protect the environment.

"I versus You" score: I: 19, You: 10

Traditional System comments

Since this letter is addressed to "Homeowner," not a person, it is obviously a mass mailing. Whittaker couldn't even be bothered to do a mail merge, which shows precisely how much they care about their customers. The opening paragraph makes it clear this letter is all about Whittaker, and the company's pride in itself is actually a turnoff because no one likes to hear anyone boast about themselves.

The third paragraph on is a heavy hitting sales pitch for their latest and probably most expensive product. Just in case you don't get the point, the company uses bolding, caps and exclamation marks so the text practically screams at you.

Whittaker says it will come to your house at no cost to you and determine if you need a new A/C system, or if you're thinking of going with someone else, they'll provide another opinion (competing bids–imagine that!)

But wait, there's more! Just in case you're not convinced to pick up the phone and call Whittaker right away, they want you to know they use ozone-friendly cooling equipment which, of course, is the norm in the industry.

Whittaker Home Comfort Company – Contrarian System

Dear Ms. Bigg,

With the crisp days of autumn rapidly approaching, you probably haven't given a thought to your home comfort system. And that's as it should be–your system should be working perfectly, and all you need to do is change the filter regularly to keep it that way.

But even so, you may be seeing your utility bills rise and in case you didn't realize it, the problem may not be with your home comfort system. There are many no-cost or low-cost ways to reduce your utility bills, which is why we'd like to offer you a free guide, "How to Keep Your Cool and Your Cash." In this handy brochure, you'll learn:

- Why using the right air filter can keep your family healthy
- Why having your home comfort system inspected twice a year can save you money year-round
- How the combination of insulation and radiant barrier in your attic can cut your costs year-round
- How to check for leaks around your windows and doors
- How your hot water heater and major appliances impact your utility bills
- When to know it's time to repair or replace your home comfort system

To get your free guide, click on the link at www.whittakerhomecomfort.com or call (972) 333-3333. We'll send your no-obligation guide right out to you, and you'll be on your way to lowering your utility bills.

And when you need service for your home comfort system or are ready to upgrade, we'll be right here, just as we have been for the last 60 years. Our team of home comfort experts can help you choose which of our products and services will best meet your family's needs–from regular system maintenance to air duct cleaning, insulation option and full system upgrades.

Ms. Bigg, thank you for considering Whittaker Home Comfort Company for your family, and I'll give you a call next week to answer any questions you may have about your current home comfort system. And remember, "When you're comfortable, you're at home with Whittaker."

Sincerely yours,
Joe Whittaker

"I versus You" score: I: 8, You: 31

Contrarian System comments

Addressed to a real person, this letter speaks to you as a homeowner. By suggesting that your home comfort system should already be working perfectly, Whittaker subtly encourages you to wonder if it really is.

Whether it is or isn't, chances are you're intrigued by the company's offer of a free, no obligation brochure that will help you save money–something you are very interested in. And because Whittaker is interested in you, you are naturally interested in Whittaker, a company you may not have heard of before but which you'll definitely keep in mind the next time your A/C needs service or a seasonal tune-up.

Finally, the president of the company assumes responsibility for following up, and even if you're not in the market for a new A/C provider, chances are that you'll tell your friends about him and his friendly company.

Abundance Bank–Traditional System

BEST BUSINESS CHECKING IN THE METROPLEX

Does your current business checking account require you to maintain certain balances to avoid fees? Wouldn't you rather have a business checking account that features no monthly maintenance fees and no minimum balance requirements?

We at Abundance Bank believe that our customers deserve superior products and services. That is why we would like to offer you our new "Advantage Business Checking" account. This new account is designed for our business customers who are tired of paying service and maintenance fees on their business accounts.

You be the judge–take a look at our new "Advantage Business Account" and see what we mean when we say that this is the best business checking account in the Metroplex:

- *No Minimum Balance*
- *No Monthly Service Charge*

- *No Per Check or Deposit Fees*
- *Free Internet Banking*
- *Free Cashier's Checks (2 per month)*
- *Free Incoming Wires*
- *Free Night Deposit Services*
- *Free Telephone Transfers*
- *Free First Order of Bank Checks (with this letter)*

We are also a preferred SBA lender and can handle most of your business and personal lending needs. I would like to tell you more about our bank and our different bank services and would like the opportunity to visit with you. Please call me at your convenience if you have any questions or would like to arrange a time to meet. I look forward to hearing from you soon.

Sincerely yours,
Donald Kiley, President

"I versus You" score: I: 14, You: 11

Traditional System comments

With a headline, no salutation and bolding, this letter comes across as junk mail. While no fees, no minimum balance, etc., is definitely appealing to some people, it may not be enough incentive for you to switch banks, especially if you have an established relationship with your current bank or if your bank already offers free checking and all the other standard perks.

But just in case you're not in the market for a new checking account, the bank's president wants your business anyway, and looks forward to hearing from you soon.

Abundance Bank–Contrarian System

Dear Mr. Bigg,

Congratulations on your new business. Whether this is your first business or your fifth, you probably have a lot of questions about what you can do to ensure it will succeed. That's why I'd like to invite you to attend, "It's Your Business," our free monthly workshop series designed to meet the special concerns of entrepreneurs like you.

In this lunch-time series, we cover such topics as:

- Why You Need a Business Plan, Even If You're Not Borrowing Money
- How to Make the Emotional Transition from Employee to Entrepreneur
- The Importance of Having a Positive Mindset in a Negative World
- Family Matters: How to Balance Home and Work
- Small Business Resources in Your Own Backyard

On Tuesday, September 9th at 11:30 AM, local CPA John Smith will be discussing, "Planning for the Tax Man: How to Shield More of Your Money." A light lunch will be provided courtesy of It Tastes Great Deli.

If you'd like to attend, please register at www.abundancebank.com/itsyourbusiness or by calling 972-517-1111. Because seats are limited, be sure to RSVP by September 3rd. At the workshop, you'll receive "Business Start-Up Basics," a handy guide full of advice and checklists prepared by Abundance Bank's Business Services department. There is no cost or obligation.

Mr. Bigg, please let me know if I can be of any service to you as you grow your business, and I'm looking forward to meeting you at the workshop.

Sincerely yours,
Donald Kiley, President

"I versus You" score: I: 7, You: 20

Contrarian System comments

If you're not already a customer of Abundance Bank, chances are that you soon will be. How could you resist an invitation to a free workshop designed to help you succeed? This letter is warm, inviting and sounds like it's written for just for you, although it is actually a template merged into a leads list the bank recently acquired of new business owners.

Notice that the letter says absolutely nothing about the bank itself; instead of pitching and hustling, the bank president is strategically planting seeds for a future relationship with you, knowing that this "it's all about you" approach really works.

The "It's Really About Me" Trap

Don't try to justify why Mr. Bigg should buy what you're selling by making your letter sound like it's about him when it's really about you. He'll know exactly what you're doing, and you'll only be fooling yourself.

This Traditional System letter was written to the vice president of sales and marketing of a global food conglomerate. The writer was the owner of a small public relations agency who intended to teach this captain of industry a thing or two about generating visibility for his products (the names have been changed, but everything else is as it was in the original letter):

Diamond Brand Foods – Traditional System

Dear Mr. Bigg,

Notice the enclosed "Food Industry Forum" article I wrote for PRO-GRESSIVE GROCER on supermarket public relations. Because the editor believed this story was useful information to readers, it was published – at no cost to me or my company.

How much did you pay for the full page, full color ad for Diamond Brand Tropical Fruits in the April issue of PROGRESSIVE GROCER? More than $11,000 – and well worth it because, as you know, this publication is one of the best in the field.

> *Advertising is very important, of course, especially for a major supermarket category like produce, fresh or canned. However, public relations as an added marketing strategy adds a significant difference, one that can substantially increase supermarket sales and penetration.*
>
> *News releases, feature stories and social media placed by a public relations counselor add a new kind of impact...credibility. Editorial write-ups have creditability! Writing and placing articles in key publications like PROGRESSIVE GROCER is just one aspect of the PR job we can do for you – and our <u>monthly</u> retainer is nowhere near $11,000. It takes quite a bit of sustained activity to reach that mark.*
>
> *Shameless Associates is a full-service agency that would bring to your program such public relations/promotional techniques as writing and media contact, direct mail, social media, producing brochures and flyers, staging promotions...and all the many details that go into public relations promotions.*
>
> *Our background includes work with organizations that target supermarkets: companies like R.T. French, Castle & Cooke, Nestle Co., and associations ranging from the American Blue Cheese Association and the California Avocado Board to the National Asparagus Association and Coffee Association.*
>
> *If you think you are not doing enough non-ad promotion of your product line, we'd love the chance to help you. Can we talk?*
>
> *Sincerely yours,*
> *Susan Shameless, President*

"I versus You" score: I: 8, You: 9

Traditional System comments

Even though this letter has more you's than I's, it's quite evident that it's all about the PR agency, not the food company. But what makes it worse is that Susan actually insults her potential client.

Although he is one of the most powerful executives in the food industry, she lets him know that advertising–*his* advertising–has no credibility, and overtly implies that the only way to get credibility for his products is by having them written up, preferably by her PR agency.

And although this food marketing expert oversees the work of dozens of marketing agencies around the world which annually spend many millions of his company's dollars on advertising, publicity and product promotion, she feels obligated to let him know that if he hired her, he could save some money.

Finally, Susan completely obliterates any credibility she might have left with Mr. Bigg by leaving the follow-up to him. Rather than the take-charge, get-things-done professional she wants him to think she is, she reveals her true self by ending her hard-charging, in-your face letter with a whimper.

Diamond Brand Foods – Contrarian System

Dear Mr. Bigg,

In a recent article in Supermarket News, you said large supermarkets are resistant to carrying local ethnic brands, despite their popularity with consumers, especially in urban markets. You said the costs involved in promoting individual local brands outweigh their potential profits, and most supermarket managers won't be bothered with brands they can't easily sell.

There's no question that getting shelf space for local ethnic packaged goods like your new specialty line, Diamond Brand Tropical Fruits, can be a challenge. But until those goods get on the shelf, there's no way of knowing how profitable they can be to the merchant, the manufacturer and you, the distributor.

And as a distributor, you know the cost-effectiveness in bundling like-kind product lines in shipping; I wondered if you've considered using the same approach to in-store promotion and merchandising.

As you can see from my website, www.ethnicfoodmktg.com, we specialize in moving ethnic goods through supermarket chains in urban, suburban and rural markets nationwide.

We've represented more than 100 local, regional and national brands from Chilean to Chinese, helping to turn previously-unknown brands into household staples through cost-effective promotional programs.

Mr. Bigg, I have some ideas that may appeal to you and your manufacturers, and I'll call you next week to discuss them with you. Thank you for your time, and I'm looking forward to speaking with you.

Sincerely yours,
Jim Stevens

"I versus You" score: I: 5, You: 13

Contrarian System comments

This letter makes it easy for Mr. Bigg to realize Jim not only has a feel for his dilemma with his ethnic products, but is already formulating strategies to move his merchandise. Notice the structure of the letter:

- *Paragraphs One and Two:* Although Jim is simply repeating what Mr. Bigg said in the article, he comes across as an expert in selling ethnic brands to supermarkets—without having to say that he was one.

- *Paragraph Three:* By briefly discussing the problem and/or opportunity Mr. Bigg faces with small ethnic brands, Jim implies he already has an understanding of Mr. Bigg's concerns.

- *Paragraph Four:* By suggesting a way to help Mr. Bigg address this issue, Jim acts as if he is already working for Mr. Bigg.

Notice that no specific ideas are given; only a vague reference to *"bundling"* and *"in-store promotion and merchandising."*

- *Paragraphs Five:* By now, Mr. Bigg is thinking, *"Who are you?"* and Jim intentionally downplays his track record to get Mr. Bigg to go to his website, which he does to learn more about the ethnic-brands expert he's going to meet.

- *Paragraphs Six:* Jim makes it very clear he expects to meet with Mr. Bigg soon and that they will be working together. By assuming responsibility for follow-up, Jim proves his company is responsible, thorough, detail-oriented and capable.

And because Jim is already mapping out a game plan for Mr. Bigg's ethnic lines so he can hit the ground selling, Mr. Bigg will have a very hard time saying "no" to an alliance with Jim.

Chapter Ten
FOLLOWING UP

All that qualifying is well and good if your First Contact was by phone, but what happens next if you did your cold calling by email or letter? Usually nothing, and this is the most frustrating part of the Traditional System sales process because you've done everything you're supposed to do, and now all you can do is wait for a response.

You figure that if Mr. Bigg doesn't contact you, it's because he's not interested in what you're offering. The sad truth is that you may never know whether he is or not because when you don't follow up, you automatically abdicate responsibility for moving the sale along.

It is your responsibility to follow up with Mr. Bigg after you've made First Contact; it is not his responsibility to follow up with you.

On the other hand, if you've sent Mr. Bigg a Contrarian System personalized sales letter that discussed his needs, concerns, issues and/or opportunities and suggested how you might help him, he's probably wondering why you haven't called him yet.

Here is where having a CRM system is essential – once you've made First Contact, you'll want to schedule a follow-up call within a week or shortly after an upcoming holiday. This way, nothing will fall through the cracks and you won't have bits of paper tacked around your computer reminding you what you should do.

Follow Through

Very often, your First Contact with Mr. Bigg will not result in an immediate sale for any number of reasons, most of which have nothing to do with you.

But that's okay, because you are forming a relationship with him, and any good relationship takes repeated contacts over time to generate a mutual sense of trust, comfort and familiarity. Depending upon the nature of your business, it could take months after First Contact before Mr. Bigg is ready to start working with you.

Meanwhile, there's a lot you can do to nurture your budding relationship with him, such as "drip" email campaigns, blogging, sending relevant articles or personalized notes, making phone calls, having informal chats and/or seeing each other at business, civic or networking events.

You need to stay in touch with Mr. Bigg, but let him tell you how and when. At the end of your First Contact or each follow-up phone call you make to him, just ask, "When should I get back with you?" and he will tell you.

Like all forms of marketing, repetition in following-up is the key, but only to an extent. For example, if you're operating a retail store or restaurant, you can connect daily with your customers through email and/or social media to promote your sales and special events, and few of them will mind.

But that same approach is totally inappropriate if you're a professional services firm, selling pricey items to other businesses or consumers where a high level of decorum is expected, or when there is a long sales cycle.

Instead, you could send a weekly or bi-weekly e-zine or article, invite selected clients to a gathering or simply call or take them to lunch every few months.

Traditional System Follow-Up

It is quite possible to take follow-up to an extreme. This is an excerpt from an article teaching recruiters how they should follow-up with their senior level corporate executive candidates:[6]

> *In many ways, a follow up call to a prospect is more challenging than a cold call. Typically, it's the follow up call that really gets the sales cycling rolling. It's here where value truly begins to manifest itself. It's here where substantive information is gathered and here is where the relationship begins to establish itself.*
>
> *That's why it is absolutely vital to have superb follow up strategies and tactics so you can make the most of the moment. Here are eight tips to making a perfect follow up call.*

Get Commitment for the Follow Up

Perhaps the single biggest mistake reps make is not establishing a specific date and time for the follow up call at the end of their initial call. Vague commitments from the prospects ("Call me next week") or the sales rep ("I'll send the proposal and follow up in a couple of days") result in missed calls, voice mail messages and ultimately a longer sales cycle.

All you need to do is simply ask for a follow up date and time. For instance, "I'll be glad to write up the proposal (quote, whatever) and email it to you. And what I would like to recommend is that we set up Tuesday, the 16th, at say, 8:45 to review it in detail and determine the next steps if any. How does that sound?"

If this is not a good time, recommend another time. If that doesn't work, get them to establish a time and date. Creating a deadline is a simple but extremely powerful tactic.

Build equity and be remembered

After every call to a first time prospect, send a thank you card. Handwrite a message on small thank you card that simply says,

"John, thank you for taking the time speaking with me today. I look forward to chatting with you further on the 16th! Kind regards." No more, no less.

In today's fast paced world, a hand written card tells the client that you took the time and the effort to do something a little different. At some level, this registers in the client's mind and creates a degree of equity in you. It differentiates you and it gets remembered. And it gives the client a reason to be there when you make you follow up call.

If you don't think a card will get there in time, send an email with the same note. Just be aware that an email does not have nearly the same impact as a handwritten note.

Email a Reminder and an Agenda

The day before your follow up call, send an email to your prospect to remind them of your appointment. In the subject line, put "Telephone appointment for August 16th and article of interest." Note that the subject line acts as a reminder but it is vague enough that the prospect will probably open it. There is a hint that maybe the date and time has changed.

Your email should confirm the date and time of the appointment and then briefly list your agenda: "John, the call should only take 10 minutes. We'll review the proposal and I'll answer any questions. And then we'll determine the next steps, if any."

Notice how the words echo the words that were used when the follow up was initially set, in particular the trigger phrase "the next steps, if any." The "if any" will help reduce some of the stress or concern a first-time prospect might have.

Often, they skip out on the follow up call because they are worried that they'll have to make a commitment. This is natural and okay. If the prospect senses an easy, informal, no pressure type of phone call, he is more likely to show up on time for that call.

Add Value in a P.S.

Notice in the subject line there is a reference to an article. At the end of your email, add a P.S. that says, "John, in the meantime, here's an article I thought you might enjoy regarding..."

The article may be about your industry, the market, a product or better yet, something non-business related that you had discussed in your initial call. This creates tremendous value even if the client does not open it because you took the time to do something extra. This helps get you remembered and gives the client yet another reason to take your follow up call.

Of course, this means you have to do some homework. Start looking on the web for articles of interest and value relative to your market, industry etc. Keep a file of these articles because they can be used over and over again.

Call on Time

Don't start your relationship on the wrong foot. Call on time. Never, ever be late with your follow up call, not even by a minute. The promptness and respect you show on a follow up call reflects on you, your company and your products.

Avoid Opening Statement Blunders

Here some of the classic follow up opening statements blunders:

> "I was calling to follow up on the proposal"
> "I am calling to see if you had any questions'
> "I just wanted to make sure you got my email"
> "The reason for my follow up was to see if you had come to decision"

It is not that these opening statements are poor, but rather that they're routine and common place; they do nothing to position you or differentiate you. What this really means is that you are perceived as yet another run of the mill vendor looking for a sale. You need a little more pizzazz.

Build a Follow-Up Opening Statement

There are four simple steps to creating that pizzazz. First, introduce yourself using your full name. Second, give your company name. Okay, so far it's pretty obvious, but it is in this step where you differentiate yourself.

Remind the client why you are calling and what prompted the follow up call in the first place. This means going back to your initial cold call and reminding the client of the "pain" or the "gain" that was discussed or hinted at in your previous call. For instance,

> "Debbie, this is Michael Powers calling from ABC Educom. Debbie, when we spoke last week you had two concerns. First, you indicated that you were concerned about having your current on-line training program renewed automatically before you had a chance to review it in detail, and second, that there were several modules whose content was questionable."

Michael reminds Debbie why she agreed to this call. He does this because he knows that clients are busy, they forget or the urgency of last week may not seem so urgent this week, so he scratches at the scab. Remind your client of the irritation and then move on to the agenda.

> "What I would like to recommend at this stage is two things. First, we review those modules that have you so concerned and second, we'll take a closer look at the current contract. Then we'll determine the next steps, if applicable. How does that sound?"

Clients like a clear, concise agenda. They want a vendor who is organized and doesn't waste their time. They want someone to takes control and move the call forward. This gives them confidence.

Finally, notice how the rep repeats a theme that he established in the first call and in his follow up email. He indicates that they will "determine the next steps if applicable." It's a nice touch and reduces client resistance.

Be Persistent, Polite and Professional, But Not a Pest

If you follow this formula, about 70% of the time the client is there. But that leaves 30% who are not for one reason or another. If the prospect is not there, leave a message so that he knows you called on time. Say,

> "Hi Debbie, it's _____ from _____ calling for our 8:45 appointment. Sounds like you might be tied up for a few moments. I'll call in 10 minutes if I haven't heard from you. In the meantime, my number is _____."

Next, call in 10 minutes exactly. If the prospect is still not there leave another message:

> "Hi Debbie, it's _____ from _____, following up on our 8:45 appointment. Looks like you're still tied up. Please give me a call when you're free at _____, otherwise I will call you later this morning or early this afternoon."

So far, you've been persistent without being a pest. Now, give the prospect a chance to call. A good rule of thumb is a half a day. Four hours is plenty of time and space for the prospect to call you and more importantly, it doesn't make you look desperate or annoying. Here's what you can say,

> "Debbie, it's _____ from _____. I called a couple of times today, but as of yet we have not been able to connect. When we last spoke, you were concerned about the contract expiry date

and the content of some of the modules. I'm sure you don't want that date to come and go. So, my number is _____."

Notice how the rep reminds the client of the call, but does not make her feel guilty or embarrassed by using the phrase "but as of yet we have not been able to connect". Also, notice that the rep reminds the client about their early talks and the "pain" the prospect was experiencing. In effect, he wants Debbie to think, "That contract is nagging me. I'd better get back to him."

If that doesn't work, make four more follow up calls but space them three business days apart. This shows persistence, but the calls are spread far enough apart that the client doesn't feel like she's being stalked. If there's no response by then, you probably won't get one, but at least you took a good stab at it.

According to one Traditional System sales pundit,[7] you're not so much following-up as you are being just shy of harassing Mr. Bigg:

For every one sales attempt, you should expect to leave at least three messages over a five day timeframe. This accomplishes three goals: it will keep your message fresh in the prospect's mind, your message will be consistent, and it will be delivered with due respect for the prospect's time.

If you don't get a response, you can drop the prospect for now, or you can repeat the 1-3-5 cycle with a different message, which means six contacts over a ten-day window. Your message is getting through and you are aggressively trying to reach the prospect without becoming a constant annoyance.

Think about it: do you want to do business with someone who scratches your scabs, reminds you of your pain, sets your agendas and practically stalks you? No? Then don't you be that person.

Remember that Mr. Bigg has a life, things change and you are just not that important to him right now. If he misses your phone appointment, doesn't return your calls or respond to your voice mails, the worst thing you can do is to keep calling, especially within a short timeframe.

Contrary to what the Traditional System will tell you, aggressive, persistent follow-up won't make you a priority; instead, it will make you a pariah. Count on it: Mr. Bigg is getting your messages but for whatever reason, is choosing not to call you back:

- He doesn't want, need or have an interest in what you're selling even though you think he should
- His plans have changed; what was urgent last month has either been taken care of or mothballed
- He feels guilty about not returning your calls and figures you'll eventually go away if he ignores you
- He's out of the office, on vacation, out sick, out of town or just too busy
- He's the wrong person to talk to and/or you have the wrong phone number

---

Your goal for your follow up calls should not be to make a sale or to get an appointment; it should be to establish a relationship with Mr. Bigg or move the one you have with him forward. Once you have a good relationship with him in place, meetings and sales will come easily and naturally.

Contrarian System Follow-Up

In most sales situations, follow-up after First Contact is 98% of the sales process, and you may encounter some or all of these issues with people not getting back to you or not being there when they said they would be.

Of course, you'd love to do business with Mr. Bigg, but whether or not he does business with you will depend a great deal on how you handle your First Contact follow-up. Remember, people do business with people they like, so when Mr. Bigg answers, you should respond without pitching, hustling or panicking, like this:

> *"Mr. Bigg, this is Mary Jonas, and I'm calling to follow up on some material I emailed you last week. Did you have a chance to look it over?"*

Chances are good that even if he got your email, he probably didn't read it and it's buried in his in-box. So treat this follow-up call exactly like a First Contact phone call, because from Mr. Bigg's perspective, that's exactly what it is (see Chapter 7).

If Mr. Bigg is unavailable, ask his assistant when you should call back, and then add a few days to that date to give him time to dig out, especially if he's been traveling or out sick for any length of time. This respects both his time and her authority to know what's going on, so when you call again, you'll get a much warmer reception.

Get Back With Me Later

Mr. Bigg may want you to get back with him tomorrow or may say, *"Call me in July"* or even *"I don't know when you should call me."* In that case, tell him you'll call him in six months, and his response will tell you if you're on the right track.

Often, the delay is due to cash flow and/or other higher-priority items, and Mr. Bigg might say, *"No, call me in two months."* In two months when you call back, he will most likely tell you exactly what's going on and how he sees you as part of his plans or when to call back again.

Don't be disappointed if your follow-up call results in another phone call later on; sales is fundamentally a wooing process and it can take months or years to build a good relationship. Every interaction you have with Mr. Bigg should make him feel good about you because if he doesn't, he'll never buy from you.

When He Still Won't Respond

But what if Mr. Bigg still won't call you back after you've done all this? Assuming he's alive, well and is the right person you need to connect with, put him on the back burner for now. Send him an email that says you've been trying to reach him, he must have a lot going on and to please let you know if you can be of any help to him. And then you should stay in touch by:

- Putting him on your email "drip" list
- Mailing him a card for his birthday/congratulations on a deal or major event in his life or business
- Setting up a Google Alert for him and his company and industry, so your generic *"Thinking of you..."* makes a much bigger impact
- Inviting him to a meeting or event you think he'd want to attend
- Asking him to participate in a survey
- Sending him an unusual gift that makes you memorable
- Hosting an event and inviting him via email and phone call
- Recommending him on LinkedIn and/or following him
- If he has a Facebook account, following him and posting on his wall
- Using him as a resource, such as including him in an article you're writing

---

The best way to keep yourself on Mr. Bigg's radar when he's not ready to buy from you is to make referrals to him. Nothing will bring you business from Mr. Bigg faster than bringing business to him.

Asking for the Meeting

Let's assume you and Mr. Bigg are having a great conversation and he's interested in knowing more about what you have and/or how you can help him. But don't expect him to say, *"Let's meet,"* although he just might. Since this is your sales call, you are responsible for seeing it through, so here are some ways to ask for the meeting:

- *"What's good for you next week?"*
- *"Would you prefer breakfast or lunch?"*
- *"I'm free Monday and Friday for lunch. Will any of those days work for you?'*

Then plug the meeting into your CRM system and depending upon your system, send Mr. Bigg an invitation email that includes where, when and why you are meeting. And don't forget to call him the day before your meeting to confirm it's still on.

Part 3:
MEETING MR. BIGG

Chapter Eleven
TRADITIONAL SYSTEM SALES MEETING

Congrats! All your hard work has paid off and you've finally gotten a face-to-face meeting with Mr. Bigg. According to the Traditional System, this is your one and probably only chance to give your pitch, make that sale and secure that new client.

In the Traditional System, the goal of a sales presentation is to persuade a person or group of people to buy what you're selling, and your first job is to convince them they have a need for it:[8]

> *Creating a successful sales pitch requires delivering a step-by-step presentation that demonstrates a problem or need, offers a generic solution, then shows how your product or service best provides that solution.*
>
> *Create an introduction for your presentation: Depending on how many people are involved in the presentation, introduce people on both sides of the table so that everyone in the room knows why everyone else is there. Thank the attendees for coming and give a broad overview of why you are all at the meeting.*
>
> *Focus on a problem or need the customer has and make it clear that your goal for the meeting is to help the client or customer, rather than beginning the presentation talking about your company's background.*
>
> *During the first part of the presentation, home in on a problem or need the customer has: Use your product's benefits to guide you in determining this. Focus on customer problems or needs such as reducing expenses, improving quality, decreasing production time or increasing sales.*

Use facts, figures and other data to support your assumptions, using charts and graphs to quickly present it. Discuss the benefits of solving the customer's problem or filling his need, such as improved profit margins, decreased worker injuries or quicker production times.

Provide a generic solution to the customer's need: for example, if a restaurant needs to reduce labor costs, installing a dishwashing machine will help do this. If a car wash requires workers to hand dry cars after they go through its machine, installing a powerful blower would eliminate the need for these workers. Use studies and industry surveys and statistics to validate your solution.

Demonstrate how your product or service best delivers the generic solution to the customer's problem: for example, compare the cost of manual dishwashing over a one-year period to the cost of buying and using a dishwashing machine, then over a period of several years. Use case studies of your customers who have solved problems with your product or service to demonstrate your product's superiority over the competition.

Re-cap the problem, the generic solution and your product or service benefits as the answer to the customer's needs: present background information on your company to show that you are legitimate, deliver what you promise and will be around to service the customer. Discuss your warranty, guarantees, pricing programs, financing options and customer service program. Take questions and answer all queries or objections.

Stand and Deliver

If you've never given a Traditional System sales presentation before, chances are that you've sat through several, and they typically fall into one of these categories:

- *The Canned Presentation:* Everything you need to know about the product–what is it, who makes it, what it does, how it works, what it costs and why you would want it–it is presented to you in a methodical, systematic and well-planned manner. When the salesperson is finished, you get to ask questions, but ideally, all of your questions should have been answered in the presentation.

- *The Planned Presentation:* If the salesperson has done their homework, they should be able to tailor their canned presentation just enough to make you think they've put together this whole presentation just for you. This kind of presentation makes you much more interested in considering buying what the salesperson is offering because you're much more engaged in the process.

- *The Audio-Visual Presentation:* Whatever A/V device is used –charts, slides, video, films, prototypes, webinars, brochures, flip charts, etc.-this is a variation of the canned presentation in which you get to watch a show of some sort and ask questions.

- *The Problem Solving Presentation:* Considered the most effective type of presentation, the salesperson customizes their talk around your specific needs, concerns and/or opportunities, based upon information you have given them and/or their own research. You're very inclined to buy whatever the salesperson suggests, but may still hesitate.

Selling the Traditional System way is bound to make any non-salesperson nervous. What if you forget to include something important? What if the equipment you're using breaks? What if they ask a question you can't answer?

What if they object to your pricing? What if after you've done your best pitch they still want to stay with the service they're using now or go with someone else? What if you can't figure out what you're doing wrong?

No matter how you slice it, a Traditional System sales presentation has one giant flaw–you're selling and Mr. Bigg knows it. Since nobody likes to be sold but everybody loves to buy, the best way to get Mr. Bigg to buy is simply to stop selling.

The Traditional System will have you believe that the sales meeting is the most important part of the sales process; this is not correct. In fact, the most important part of the sales process is First Contact, because that first encounter will set the stage for a mutually-beneficial professional relationship–or not.

> *Mr. Bigg has a problem and to a very large degree, he already believes you can help him solve it. If he didn't believe that, he wouldn't be wasting his time talking to you.*

So relax. Just by getting the meeting with Mr. Bigg, you're halfway home to making a sale.

What Your Meeting is Really About

Once you realize that Mr. Bigg is already interested in what you have, there is no reason for you to be anxious. You have your pick of potential clients, but Mr. Bigg is in a bind and, contrary to what the Traditional System will tell you, he just doesn't have much of a choice who he can hire to help him solve his problem.

Unless you are providing a product or service where you have many colleagues in your area who do exactly what you do exactly the same way you do it for around the same price, there just aren't that many local, available, qualified people at any given time who:

- Can do what Mr. Bigg needs done
- Mr. Bigg knows about that he can contact and who he trusts to do it right
- Are aware that Mr. Bigg has a need for their products or services or
- Have the wherewithal to contact Mr. Bigg on their own

And if you are providing a product or service where you have many colleagues in your area who do exactly what you do exactly the same way you do it for around the same price, then this meeting takes on even more significance.

Like any blind date, the sole purpose of your meeting with Mr. Bigg is to determine if the two of you like each other as people, sort out the details of what he needs or wants and what you have, and mutually decide if there's enough common ground to move forward.

No matter how good or cost-effective your product or service is, no matter what great testimonials you have or what phenomenal credentials your company has, if Mr. Bigg doesn't like you, he's not going to work with you.

And if you don't like him—no matter how much you need his business—you shouldn't work with him. That's because if your budding professional relationship doesn't work at the outset, it will only get worse with time.

Chapter Twelve
CONTRARIAN SYSTEM SALES MEETING

This is the technique I have used for decades that has enabled me to walk into a meeting with a potential client and walk out with the business. It's easy, simple, enormously fun and it works. But first, there are a few things you need to do before you meet Mr. Bigg:

- *Do your homework*: Go over what you have learned about Mr. Bigg personally and professionally, his industry, his company, and particularly his problem and/or area of opportunity you have identified.

- *Get your thinking straight*: You are there to help Mr. Bigg solve his problem, not to make a sale. The sale will happen automatically once Mr. Bigg realizes you can help him get what he wants.

- *Remember that you have nothing to lose*: If Mr. Bigg or you chose not to work together, oh, well. There are plenty of other Mr. Biggs for you to call on.

- *Remember that you have nothing to prove*: Mr. Bigg already knows as much about your company, product or service as he needs to at this point; now it's a matter of personalities and details.

Begin the Conversation

It is essential to remember that you-not Mr. Bigg-are in charge of this meeting, and the key is never to let Mr. Bigg know it. As you walk in the door, there will be a greeting and a bit of small talk. If Mr. Bigg offers you a beverage, accept it even if you don't want it, don't like it and aren't thirsty.

When you accept a beverage, you instantly change the dynamics of the meeting; rather than being potential buyer and seller, Mr. Bigg is now a gracious host and you are his guest. Take a sip (or pretend to), and then put it someplace where you can't possibly spill it. That way, you have acknowledged Mr. Bigg's gift of the drink and can focus on him and not it.

Small Talk is Huge

This initial part of the meeting is typically overlooked by the Traditional System, but it's a critical element in building that warm bond you want to have with Mr. Bigg. Assuming you two have never met before, you need to find some common ground to break the ice, so look around his office; there's bound to be something you can comment on.

Look for personal items such as pictures, drawings or mementos. When I was selling patient care equipment, one dealer I called on had drawings of ducks and duck hunting scenarios lining his office walls. It was a no brainer to figure out what his passion was.

Another dealer had filled his office with dozens of small, taxidermied creatures of the forest he had shot on his ranch, he very proudly told me. A third dealer had painted the back wall of his office as an undersea landscape. It wasn't surprising to learn he was a passionate scuba diver.

> *The whole idea of this meeting is to get Mr. Bigg to like you, and there's no better way to do than to be–or pretend to be–interested in what he's interested in.*

Pull the Trigger

Now the pleasantries are over and you're both ready to get down to business. But instead of launching into a sales talk, begin the conversation by asking Mr. Bigg a "trigger question" or make a "trigger statement" that will get him talking.

Trigger questions or statements should be based upon your research and knowledge about Mr. Bigg, his company, industry or situation, and sound something like:

- To a magazine editor: *"That recent story you ran on college entrepreneurs was terrific. Did you get a chance to try out some of their products?"*
- To a commercial real estate developer (pointing to a rendering of a new project): *"What a great looking building. How's the leasing going?"*
- To a commercial interior design firm: *"It seems every time I open a paper, I read about hospitals expanding or new clinics being built. No wonder you've focused on this market."*
- To a financial services director: *"I read many new businesses are started by people in their 40's, 50's and 70's. What a unique opportunity you have with them."*

The Sound of Silence

Now don't say another word; just sit there with a slight smile and wait for Mr. Bigg to respond, although he probably won't. Chances are he has never had a salesperson talk so intelligently about his business before, and he will be shocked into silence.

This silence will probably last only a few minutes, but it may seem like hours. Regardless of how long it lasts or how strongly you feel the urge to say something – *don't!*

Just sit there and wait for him to talk first; eventually, he will. This is critical to your staying in control of the meeting because when you create a silence, the person who speaks first loses.

Get Mr. Bigg talking and keep him talking about whatever he wants to talk about for as long as he wants to talk about it because the more he talks, the more likely it is he will talk himself right into buying whatever you are selling.

When Mr. Bigg starts to talk, he will launch into a monologue about himself, his family, company or situation. Take out a pad and start taking notes; these notes are very important and you will need them later.

Regardless of what Mr. Bigg talks about, there will come a point when he will bring up whatever is most important to him. This is the real reason you are meeting with him, whether either of you knew it when you two arranged the meeting.

When I was recruiting clients as a commercial real estate publicist, I would walk in, ask a trigger question or make a trigger statement, shut up, and allow Mr. Bigg talk first. Prompted by the silence, he'd start talking, continue to talk for 20 minutes (I have timed it), and finally say something like:

"Now, Janet, when we have you working for us, the first thing we'll need you to do is _____." or "Our biggest problem with publicity is getting included in articles. Can you do that?"

The beautiful part of this scenario was that I never mentioned what I did, what I've done or what I could do for him. I didn't have to.

This Stuff Works #1

In the late 1990s when I was a commercial real estate writer and publicist, I was used to dealing with sophisticated companies at the upper edge of the industry. My targeted clients had to have a corporate structure, deep financial pockets, a large, national, commercial real estate portfolio and be based in Dallas where I lived.

There were only a few companies that met my criteria, and the number 2 man at one of them agreed to see me. "Fred" headed the company's multi-family development and management division, which had one of the largest apartment portfolios in the country at the time.

I had previously worked with Allegiance Realty Group, one of Fred's biggest colleagues in the industry, which had since been sold to another company and merged into oblivion, so I was familiar with the kinds of publicity issues Fred's company was most likely facing. Having Fred's company as a client seemed a natural fit.

My research about Fred's company merely involved reading the very trade magazines I was writing for. I realized that despite its size and importance, Fred's company was virtually invisible when it came to exposure within the industry, and that meant opportunity for both of us.

Getting the meeting took some doing because Fred was traveling extensively, and I finally got my meeting after weeks of stalls and rescheduling through his secretary. But since he and I had never spoken, I didn't know why Fred had agreed to see me.

In my letter to Fred, I explained that as a publicist, I had noticed his company was conspicuously absent in trade articles, industry reviews, opinion roundtables and panels at industry conferences. If his firm was anything like Allegiance Realty Group, I assumed that Fred was going after third-party portfolio assignments from institutional owners like banks, insurance companies and pension funds.

Working under this assumption, I suggested to Fred that perhaps a bit of visibility in the trade press might help land some of these large accounts. Clearly, I had touched a nerve since he agreed to see me, but I didn't know if my assumption was true or whether there was something else he needed help with.

After we shook hands, Fred apologized for the scheduling delays, saying he didn't get a chance to read my brochure because he had just returned from a three-week trip.

We sat down with me on the sofa and him in a large, plush, executive chair. Right there on his desk was his open briefcase with my brochure sticking up out of it which he hadn't read but had carried around for three weeks.

As we settled in, Fred leaned back in his chair, crossed his arms and legs, smiled and said, *"I suppose you're here to tell me what you can do for me."* Clearly, this was an invitation for me to launch into a sales presentation, but I knew that would be a mistake for two reasons:

- Fred's body language was speaking volumes: he was leaning away from me and had crossed his arms and legs, mentally and physically raising a wall of resistance, and

- I didn't know what he needed, so doing a *"Here's What I Do and Why You Should Hire Me"* commercial would be like throwing spaghetti against the wall and hoping some of it sticks.

Besides, in the nine years I had been in business, I had never done a sales presentation for anyone and I wasn't about to do one for him. I merely would go in, ask questions, actively listen, encourage Mr. Bigg to do all of the talking and wait for the inevitable *"yes."* This approach had always worked; Fred would be no different.

But the first thing that had to happen was that Fred's wall of resistance had to come down; I decided to shatter it instead. So, rather than allowing this meeting to be about my company, I turned it around and made it about his company by saying, *"Actually, I'm here to listen. I want you to tell me how you think I can help you achieve your goals."*

Fred's reaction was dramatic and instantaneous: his arms and legs flew apart, and he sat on the edge of his seat leaning forward with his eyes popping and his mouth hanging open. He had never gotten such a response from a vendor before, and his wall of resistance had simply vaporized. Fred was open, receptive and intrigued; *now* we could have our meeting.

We sat in total silence for about three minutes when the pressure finally got to him, and Fred began to talk. He described how the company grew from a small, local property partnership to a national, mega-conglomerate with interests in every facet of commercial real estate.

He was right in the middle of discussing their industrial portfolio when he hit that magic 20-minute mark and as if on cue, it happened. Completely out of the blue, totally off topic and from nowhere, Fred said, *"One of the things I'm most proud of is our work in technology."*

He got up, walked over to his computer, and showed me version 1.0 of a proprietary software program the company had built for its own portfolio. As I looked at it, I realized I was probably the first person outside the company to see this thing.

Being a non-techie, I couldn't care less about software, but since this was obviously important to Fred, it immediately became important to me.

It was easy to see from Fred's excitement that this software program was more than just a company project; it was his personal baby. So, I started treating him like the proud papa of a newborn, oooing and ahhing over his pride and joy:

"Would you look at that? Isn't that incredible! What else does it do? Have you made this available to your third-party owners? What do your managers think?"

The more I raved about his wonderful new software program, the more Fred beamed, so I poured it on. He then turned to me and said, *"You know, we really need to tell people in the industry about this. You could do that for us, couldn't you?"*

"Oh, yes," I said. Fred got up, and smiling as he walked to his desk he said, *"I suppose when you walked in here, you didn't know you*

were walking out with two jobs, did you?" Realizing he was teasing me because he was feeling good about hiring me, I went along with the joke, looked around and said, *"Did I miss something?"*

Fred handed me a piece of paper saying, *"I was going to do this, but I think I'll let you handle it."* I walked out of that office with two projects after an hour and a half with a man known to be impossible just to get in front of. And in all that time, I never said one word about me.

Take the Tour

In the Traditional System, your sales meeting occurs in isolation behind a closed door, and you are shut off from everything and everyone else in the company. But if you want to show Mr. Bigg you are really interested in helping him solve his problem, ask him to take you on a tour of the office, facility, store or plant, or if you're in a consumer's home and if it's appropriate, compliment them on it and ask to see it.

Mr. Bigg should be flattered you asked and glad to show you around, either right then or on your next visit, especially if this is a business-to-business call. If he declines for any reason, this is a clear sign he's not convinced you're the right provider for him or he's not the right client for you. Should this happen, graciously end the meeting, leave and be grateful you found out now that the vibes simply weren't right.

During the tour, Mr. Bigg should be doing nearly all of the talking, especially about his company, its projects and its plans. Encourage him to keep talking about whatever is important to him, and be an interested, engaged listener, even if you have to fake it.

There is a very good chance that during your tour you will meet "Charlie," one of Mr. Bigg's employees; you are "Diane." Out of sheer politeness, Mr. Bigg will be inclined to introduce you:

> Mr. Bigg: *"Charlie, I want you to meet Diane. Diane's going to be helping us with our new program."*
> You: *"Nice to meet you, Charlie."*

Congratulations, you have just made your sale. Wasn't that easy?

By greeting Charlie, you have acknowledged that Mr. Bigg and you will be doing business together, and Mr. Bigg, who is applauding himself on his ability to spot great talent, proceeds to introduce you to more of the people you may or may not ever deal with.

If Mr. Bigg takes you around and does not introduce you to other people, this is a very good indication he's not that serious about working with you. Chances are, you were probably not that serious about him either, so it's no loss. But the odds are in your favor that if you go on a tour and keep Mr. Bigg talking about himself and his company, you'll go home with a new client.

The Group Presentation

Just like the dreaded job panel interview, the Traditional System will have you believe that doing a sales presentation before a group of strangers is a nerve-wracking experience:[9]

> *Make no mistake. The initial sales presentation in front of a panel is one of the hardest sales calls you will ever make. Here are five reasons why it's hard:*
>
> - *Prospects act differently when they are part of a panel. Members of a panel are more conservative, reserved and difficult to engage. The decision makers on a panel will rarely exert their power while receiving a presentation and the underlings are very unlikely to step up to ask questions or make comments.*
>
>   *While a seller may have developed a relationship with one of the panel members during previous meetings, that panel member is likely to shrink into the background so as not to appear biased in favor of one presentation team.*

- *A panel typically includes out-of-towners. Folks fly into town to be a part of a panel because they believe they'll learn more by seeing face-to-face presentations. The problem is that the travelers are out of sorts. They are thinking about people back at home or at the home office. They are thinking about the fact that they forgot their favorite shoes or that they didn't bring work-out clothes. In short, they are distracted.*

- *A panel sees a lot of presentations. The purpose of a panel is to get all the decision makers together and view presentations from all the competing vendors. By seeing everyone in a day or two, panels hope to come to informed decisions. Unfortunately, all those presentations end up blending together and a typical panel is unable to say which idea was presented by whom.*

- *Panels don't have much time. We are usually asked to make a presentation in half of our usual time. This is virtually impossible because we have prepared so completely that we have even more to say than usual. We've included pictures and video and creative ideas that the panel asks us to e-mail to them after the meeting. The resulting presentation appears rushed and incomplete–because it is.*

- *We act differently in front of a panel, too. Most of us, who are fine in front of a person or two, act much more nervously in front of a panel. Our nervousness makes us more reserved and we become less interesting. Less interesting people tend to blend together in the mind of a panel.*

    Typically, we attempt to combat the effects of a panel presentation by preparing more completely than usual. Unfortunately, some of our extra work actually contributes to a less than positive experience.

    Here's something to consider: the next time you have to make a presentation in front of a panel, prepare the content as usual and then set it aside. Spend time practicing the dynamics of making the presentation. What you must do is to make an indelible impression on the panel. Here are five ideas on how to do it:

- *Bring refreshments:* If your meeting is at 3 p.m. then bring coffee, but don't just bring cups of coffee. Roll in a cart with an expresso machine or bring a barista to prepare specialty drinks. If you are first up in the morning, bring a tray of pastries the size of a mountain.

- *Prepare your anecdotes:* Perhaps you have a forty-five second story that segues nicely into reasons why the prospect should hire you, or if you know the children of one of the panel members you might prepare a fun, relatable story about one of your children of a similar age.

  The point is to have a couple of these stories in your hip pocket that you can use at the beginning of the presentation to get the panel to pay attention to you and remember you.

- *Dress in character:* This might be especially difficult for some as it calls attention to yourself in a way that is dramatically different than usual. Of course, that is the point. If your presentation, includes information about a Cinco de Mayo promotion, you might dress as a Mexican soldier.

- *Bring a celebrity:* Does your presentation include something about sports? Bring an athlete with you. Ideally, the athlete is dressed as his athletic self and not his street self. Don't think you know a celebrity who would go with you? You'd be surprised at who you know who goes to the same gym as one of your local athletes.

- *Stand and deliver:* When invited to sit, let the panel know that you prefer to stand. Standing allows you to peer over the top of the laptops shielding the panel from your influence. Standing allows you to move around which forces the panel to watch you.

In the fierce world of big-ticket professional corporate selling, perhaps some of these tactics may work. But when you're doing a panel presentation to small companies, forget about the hoopla and just focus on the reason you're there.

This Stuff Works #2

When I was the public relations consultant for Allegiance Realty Group in the mid-1990s, I was a member of the panel which was to choose a vendor for the company's logo.

Allegiance was the merger between Balcor Property Management, an East Coast apartment leasing/management company and Tishman West, a West Coast office, industrial and retail leasing/management company, and a new logo was part of its rebranding.

The meeting was held in Atlanta, and most of the panel members were from out of town. There were two local contenders for the job – a very large, full-service advertising agency that had been in business for decades, and a two-person design firm that was barely out of the starting gate. From all outward appearances, it looked like Goliath was going to cream David.

First up was the advertising agency which had brought four people, two of whom never said a word. The agency's senior executive proceeded to launch into a commercial, proudly boasting about his company's work with corporations, government agencies and non-profits.

If his intent was to impress us with his company's credentials, it had the just opposite effect; we wondered if he knew anything about the commercial real estate industry, which he never once mentioned.

Then the ad agency's art director spoke, and it was clear he hadn't put much thought into his presentation either. The mandate to both firms was to design a logo using the capital letter "A" as its basis.

But as the art director walked around the room, he flipped through dozens of pages of hastily-drawn large and small "a's," literally ripping them out of his sketch book, saying, *"Here, take a look at this one. You don't like this one? How about this one ...?"*

After lunch, it was the design firm's turn. I was really looking forward to their presentation because what no one else on the panel knew was that the president of the design firm had called me the week before the meeting to learn about Allegiance and what we wanted the logo to do for us; in other words, he did his homework. I was so impressed by his initiative that I was determined to help him win our business.

About six months before this meeting, a New York-based international commercial real estate company had undergone a major rebranding, complete with a new name, logo and positioning. This was huge news within the industry, and I told the president of the design firm to discuss the rebranded company and their marketing challenges in his presentation to us because the other members of the panel would know what he was talking about.

Sure enough, he did, and when he said the rebranded company's name and discussed how Allegiance was facing similar marketing issues, the other members of the panel physically jolted. Not only did they know exactly what he was talking about, they couldn't believe their ears.

This boutique design firm president had detailed knowledge about something no one outside the commercial real estate industry should know or care about, yet he was speaking about it as if he was an industry insider. It would be an understatement to say they were impressed; in fact, they were floored.

Then the design firm's art director got up to speak. He walked over to a large flip chart, opened the cover sheet, and revealed the most incredible, full-color variation on the capital letter "A" we had ever seen; we literally gasped.

The art director began his talk by apologizing; because of deadlines for other clients, he hadn't had much time and was up until two in the morning working on our logo. All we could think was, *"Holy Cow! He did that at two in the morning?"*

He then took us visually step-by-step through the evolution of the logo, discussing the design and thought process behind each stage and the logic ingrained in the final result. We were captivated and enthralled, and our decision to hire him and his partner was unanimous. The big agency told us later they thought they had us nailed, but in reality, they didn't stand a chance.

This Stuff Works #3

When I was applying to be Allegiance's PR consultant, I was to meet with the heads of the company's four divisions from around the country and two local senior-level field people in a single meeting. The Chicago-based CEO was not there, but would agree to whatever the group recommended.

The executives were in Dallas for a corporate meeting, and I was to meet them for dinner after their business day was over. Two of the executives lived locally, so they asked me to meet them at a nearby pizza restaurant (yes, really).

I sat at the corner of the table facing the heads of the office, apartment, industrial and retail divisions – four different kinds of income-producing, investment-grade properties, none of which had anything in common with the other.

As we were being served our food, one of the executives said, *"So, Janet, how would you market our company?"* That, of course, was, *"Tell me about yourself,"* which would make the meeting about me. Now, there was no way I was going to answer that question, especially with plate of steaming lasagna in front of me.

Instead, I looked at each respective division head in turn and said, *"As you know, marketing an apartment property is completely different from marketing an office building, which is totally different from promoting a shopping center, which is completely unlike leasing up an industrial park."* In turn, each division head nodded in agreement.

I then steered the conversation back where it belonged – on them, their properties, Balcor's recent merger with Tishman West and their desire to pursue third-party property management assignments. And the next day, the panel informed the CEO that by unanimous vote, I was their new publicist.

Chapter Thirteen
HANDLING QUESTIONS AND OBJECTIONS

This is the part of selling that gives even seasoned professional salespeople pause. But like every other part of the sales process, handling questions and objections effectively isn't a matter of technique; it's a matter of tact.

Traditional Barriers to Buying

In the Traditional system, objections are obstacles and are to be expected as a natural part of making the sale. Salespeople are taught that unless those objections are addressed, overcome or maneuvered around, the sale is never going to happen:[10]

> *Most salespeople think of objections as a bad thing, but they're missing the big picture. If your prospect raises an objection, that's actually a good sign. The fact that they're talking out their concern means that they're giving you a chance to answer it.*
>
> *If someone is completely uninterested in buying your product, they won't bother to object – generally they'll just sit through your presentation in silence (with arms folded) and then send you away. Here's a simple process to help resolve your prospect's objections:*
>
> - *Listen to the objection: Don't jump all over the prospect as soon as he says, "But what about ..." Give him a chance to explain exactly what's bothering him. Don't just tune him out, either – listen. You*

can pick up some really valuable clues from the way a prospect phrases his objection.

- *Say it back to the prospect:* When you're absolutely sure the prospect is done talking, look thoughtful for a moment and then repeat back the gist of what he's said. Something like, "I see you're concerned about maintenance costs" is fine. This both shows that you were listening and gives him a chance to clarify. "Well, it's not so much the cost I'm worried about as the downtime."

- *Explore the reasoning:* Sometimes the first objections aren't the prospect's real concern. Many prospects don't want to admit that they don't have enough money to buy your product, so they'll raise a host of other objections instead.

  Before you launch into answering an objection, ask a few exploratory questions, like "Is product downtime a particular issue? Have you had trouble with it before?" Draw the prospect out a bit.

- *Answer the objection:* Once you understand the objection completely, you can answer it. When a customer raises an objection, they're actually expressing fear. Your task at this point is to relieve their fears. If you have specific examples, such as a story from an existing customer or a few statistics, by all means present them–hard facts make your response stronger.

- *Check back with the prospect:* Take a moment to confirm that you've answered the prospect's objection fully. Usually this is as simple as saying, "Does that make sense?" or "Have I answered your concern?"

- *Redirect the conversation:* If you're in the middle of your presentation when the prospect raises his objection, once you've answered it, quickly summarize what you'd been talking about before you *move on. If you've finished your pitch, check if the prospect has any other objections and then start closing the sale.*

Imagine for a moment that you are Mr. Bigg and are considering buying something non-critical but important or desirous for yourself, your family, your home or your business. While salesman Bob is explaining what he has and why you would want it, you bring up several objections:

- Price: *"The price is too high"* or *"We can't afford it"*
- Authority: *"I have to talk to my spouse/advisor/partner about this"*
- Need: *"We're happy with what we're using now"*
- Timeliness: *"We want to wait on this"*
- Value: *"I need to think about it"*

Ever the Traditional System salesman, Bob has anticipated your objections and has his answers ready:[11]

- *Price: Instead of focusing on the product's cost, Bob emphasizes its value and gives specific examples of how it will solve your problem.*

- *Authority: Rather than seeing this as a dismissal ploy, Bob tries to get you and the other person together in the room or on a joint phone call so he can identify your underlying concerns and address those specific issues.*

- *Need: Bob knows that complacency is often a result of being ill-informed about a problem or opportunity, so he describes the overarching problem or opportunity in depth.*

  He brings up examples or case studies of families or businesses similar to yours who have made some recent changes similar to the one he is suggesting. He also knows that fear of change is a natural reaction, so he does his best to calm your concern by showing examples of positive change to provide a boost of confidence.

- *Timeliness:* Bob hates this objection more than anything, so he strives to make it so compelling for you to buy right now that if you don't, you'll feel as if you'll regret passing up this once-in-a-lifetime opportunity. To do this, he simplifies the buying process, laying out attractive terms that are only available in a very specific window of time.

- *Value:* Bob realizes that despite everything he's said up to this point, you just aren't convinced to buy from him and/or buy from him right now, so he attempts to build credibility with you.

  He reminds you of the specific features of the product that address your needs and introduces guarantees or return policies or other benefits that demonstrate value and help to build your trust.

The Traditional System's way of handling objections puts you on the defensive—the best you can hope for is to neutralize Mr. Bigg's resistance and somehow convince, coerce or cajole him into changing his mind. And if he doesn't, you have failed.

This kind of selling is enough to give anyone heartburn. Fortunately, you don't have to go through it.

Objections Overruled

When you are talking with Mr. Bigg about his needs, interests and concerns and he brings up an issue that sounds like a *"no,"* much of the time it is actually a *"yes"* in disguise. Far from being obstacles, objections are actually buying signals because Mr. Bigg has to be interested in what you are offering him in order to have objections.

> *The Traditional System assumes Mr. Bigg is not interested in what you're selling, which automatically moves him to "no" even before you contact him. But the Contrarian System assumes Mr. Bigg is interested in what you're selling, so he is already at "yes" before you contact him.*

As a result, the angst, anguish and turmoil in the Traditional System of selling are dramatically minimized or simply don't exist in the Contrarian System.

The most astonishing aspect of the Contrarian System is that as Mr. Bigg talks, he will bring up–and override–his own objections all by himself. All you have to do is sit there and listen as he decides to buy what you're selling:

- *Price/Value:* Mr. Bigg will justify out loud that the value of having what you're selling far outweighs the cost of getting it.

- *Authority:* Since Mr. Bigg has convinced himself to move ahead, he'll persuade anyone else who may be involved to go along with him. As far as he's concerned, it's a done deal.

- *Need:* Mr. Bigg will remind himself how much he wants and/or needs it and how much he's looking forward to having it.

- *Timeliness:* If the timing isn't right for Mr. Bigg, he will say so, and in the next breath tell you when the timing will be right and what, if anything, he needs from you or what he will do in the meantime.

And when you walk out of the meeting either with a sale or the promise of one by a certain date, not only will you be a happy camper, so will Mr. Bigg. You won't have sold him a thing; he will have bought, and you'll both get what you want.

How to Deal With Objections

For the sake of argument, let's assume you have given Mr. Bigg a Traditional System sales pitch and he throws an objection at you that you weren't expecting. You could improvise or even stall, but the best way to respond to an objection is not to respond at all.

Rather than immediately responding an objection, pause, take a deep breath, smile, and ask Mr. Bigg to clarify his objection. This is very important because what you're hearing may be completely different from what he's saying, and his objection is probably irrelevant anyway.

Let's say Mr. Bigg says, *"You don't offer the services we need."* The "qualifications/experience" issue is utterly ridiculous when you think about it. If you can't do what he needs to be done, why did he agree to see you? Has he nothing better to do than meet with unqualified vendors he has no intention of using?

So rather than you having to explain why you're wasting Mr. Bigg's time when you don't have what he wants, now he has to explain why he's wasting your time when he knew all along you didn't have what he wanted.

The best way to respond to any kind of objection is to turn Mr. Bigg's statement into a question; if he asks a question, reply with a question. Do not answer or acknowledge that the objection has any validity.

Mr. Bigg: *"We want something smaller."*
You: *"What do you mean by smaller?"*

Mr. Bigg: *"I don't think this is what we want."*
You: *"What exactly do you want?"*

Mr. Bigg: *"I want to think about it."*
You: *"What's causing your hesitation?"*

Mr. Bigg: *"Your delivery is too slow."*
You: *"How quickly do you need this?"*

By the time Mr. Bigg is done providing the answers to his own objections, both of you will know whether or not what you have is really what he wants or needs, and if it's not, the worst that happens is that you've made a great impression on him.

Because of that, don't be surprised when future sales–and those precious referrals–come from Mr. Bigg if he decides to buy from someone else at the moment.

Money Matters

Regardless of the price of what you're selling, Mr. Bigg will probably object to it. This is only human nature; why should he pay more for something if he could get away with paying less?

Any objection you get about money is probably false.

Chances are your prices are slightly more than what Mr. Bigg says he can afford, but don't you believe it. Aren't the lights on? Aren't his bills being paid? If he runs a company, aren't there people walking around and aren't the phones ringing? If Mr. Bigg is a consumer, doesn't he pay his rent or make mortgage payments and drive a car?

Do you really believe those few extra dollars are going to push him, his family or company into bankruptcy? Would you want to have a client who is so close to the brink of financial disaster? No? Then it's safe to assume Mr. Bigg has or can get the money. The issue then is not the money; the issue is getting him to spend the money on what you're selling.

It Costs How Much?

When was the last time you paid more for something than you should have, but you didn't mind because you thought you were getting a bargain or you wanted or needed it right then?

This tendency to ignore the price tag when you want something immediately is the difference between cost and value. *Cost* is what something is worth to people who don't care; *value* is what something is worth to you at a particular moment in time.

The whole point of the Contrarian System is to get Mr. Bigg to want what you're selling, because when he wants it, he will meet your price.

A great example of cost vs. value is in the movie *Jerry Maguire*. Jerry is a sports agent who gets fired and loses all of his clients except one – a short, lightweight, pompous football player who thinks he's God's gift to the game and especially to his team, Arizona.

Because his contract is about to expire and he doesn't want to become a free agent, he tells Jerry to get him a $10 million renewal, multi-year contract. But the team's owner has a different idea.

He tells Jerry the football player isn't worth the $1.1 million he's now getting and what's more, when his contract is up, he's going to be dropped from the team.

Near the end of the movie is the NFL playoff game with Arizona needing one touchdown to win. As the clock ticks away the last few minutes of the game, the football player does an incredible, impossible leap to catch the ball, flips and lands on his back, knocking himself momentarily unconscious.

The medics rush to the field and the silent crowd is on its feet; even the television reporters covering the game speak in hushed tones. It's a first: Arizona is going to the Super Bowl, but at this moment, nobody cares.

And then, miraculously, the football player wakes up unhurt. Lying on the ground hidden from view by the medics, he realizes he is the newest star of Big League football and springs to his feet, celebrating his victory along with millions of cheering fans.

His reward is a four-year renewal contract with Arizona worth $11.2 million. Far from being upset, the Arizona team owner is now happy to be paying ten times what he was paying before for the exact same football player.

But nothing about the football player has changed; he's still short, lightweight, mediocre and now even more pompous than ever. The only thing that has changed is that in the eyes of the team owner, the football player's value as a contributing member of the team has skyrocketed.

Before the game, the team owner thought only in terms of the football player's cost to him. But with the football player now the MVP who took his team to the Super Bowl, you can imagine the team owner is thinking:

"I now have the hottest player in the league and his contract is just about up. If he becomes a free agent, he'll be worth at least $15 million, so I'll low-ball him at $11 million and see what happens."

What happens is that everyone wins: the football player gets the money he wants and a new contract with the team of his choice, Jerry gets a cool $1 million commission, is instantly the hottest sports agent in town and is saved from bankruptcy, and the team owner gets his prized player at a discount.

We're In the Money

In the Traditional System, you're supposed to defend your position, justify your reasoning and explain why your product or service is worth the money you are charging:

Mr. Bigg: *"Your price is too high."*

> You: *"The value of this product far exceeds its cost over time. Your investment will more than pay for itself because of its superior workmanship, extended warrantee and 24/7 customer service. Many of our clients in your industry have found cost savings to exceed 40% over three years ..."*

But when you use the Contrarian System, you know that any money objection Mr. Bigg gives you is false; all you have to do is make him prove it.

Handle money objections like any other objection–just turn the statement or question into a question. Do not answer, respond or validate his objection in any way.

Mr. Bigg: *"Your price is too high."*
You: *"What do you mean, 'too high'"?*

Now just sit there silently and wait for Mr. Bigg to respond. Don't say a word; just allow the pressure of the silence to do its work. When Mr. Bigg finally speaks, he will attempt to defend his reasons for trying to not pay a fair price for the item he wants or needs, explain how his company can't afford your product or justify the company's rigid annual budget, which he neglected to mention before and over which he has total control.

Then the two of you can discuss what Mr. Bigg expects to receive for the money he's going to pay for your product or service, and at that point, you can decide whether it's worth your time to continue the conversation.

If Mr. Bigg gives you a hard time about the money as he's deciding whether he wants to do business with you, imagine how difficult he would be as a client.

Mr. Bigg: *"Your price is too high."*
You: *"How much do you think having your problem solved is worth?"*

Mr. Bigg: *"Would you be willing to offer me a discount to do business with you?"*
You: *"Does your doctor offer you a discount in order to do business with him?"*

Mr. Bigg: *"I can get the same thing cheaper."*
You: *"What is more important to you – the price of the item or the value of what it can do for you?"*

Mr. Bigg: *"We're speaking to other providers who are willing to accept less than you are to do business with us."*
You: *"If you were offered an opportunity to work with a client who paid you less for the same work than you could get from working with somebody else, would you take it?"*

If Mr. Bigg can't afford to work with you, you can't afford to work with him. Any discount you offer to get his business will cost you far more in time, energy and angst than what little money you may eventually collect from him.

When it comes to negotiating, don't ever be afraid to ask for what you want; even if you think you're making an outlandish request; it may not seem outlandish to Mr. Bigg at all. The worst that can happen is you get a *"no"* to some items, but you know Mr. Bigg wants what you have (if he didn't, he wouldn't be negotiating with you), and deals are rarely lost over minor points.

You're not being greedy or selfish when you ask for what you want, and Mr. Bigg knows this; you just want to be fairly compensated for providing something that will benefit him, his family and/or his company. After all, that's exactly what he expects when he sells something.

Asking Ain't Getting

Selling is the process of asking. The bad news about asking is that if you ask enough people or the same people enough times, most of them will eventually say *"no."* The good news about asking is that if you ask enough people or the same people enough times, most of them will eventually say *"yes."*

But asking requires you take a risk, which is the fear that someone or something is dangerous, may cause you pain or is a threat, or that you will be repulsed, ridiculed or disliked. In selling, this risk is called "rejection."

In business, a fear of rejection translates into a belief that people you don't yet know and who don't yet know you or how you can help them get what they want, won't do business with you. It's not rejection you fear; it's the consequences of what might happen if too many people keep saying "no."

The Traditional System has all kinds of ways to help you cope with and work through your fear of rejection, but they all boil down to "grow up and get over it":[12]

> *No matter what sales process you have in place, the irrational fear of rejection is a major obstacle to success in sales. The simple act of picking up the phone, calling or meeting a new customer is a gut wrenching experience for most salespeople. Many ultimately fail because their fear has crippled them from moving through the sales process.*
>
> *Rejection is tough to deal with, but it simply is part of sales. Changing your thinking and developing a new and different perspec-*

tive are the keys to overcoming the fear of rejection. As soon as you identify the mental programming that lies at the core of your fear, you can begin to question it, challenge it and find experiences that contradict it.

Unmanaged fear destroys success, and great salespeople aggressively work to eliminate fear. The only limits to your sales success are the ones you impose on yourself. The competition is in your own mind. When you do what you fear; the fear fades away and success appears.

How you handle rejection is simply a matter of perspective. Remember, every salesperson gets rejected, every one of them. Big deal. Move on, suck it up and go sell something. Remember, it's not what you sell, it's how you sell.

I Said No!

Are you tired of hearing *"no"*? Guess what? You say it all the time:

- *"I'm too busy"*
- *"I'm not interested"*
- *"I'm just looking"*
- *"That's not what I'm looking for"*
- *"Take me off your email list"*
- *"No, thanks"*

When you say *"no"* to other people, do they cringe, hide in the corner, give up trying because it's pointless to go on, or claim they're no good? No? Well, why should you?

Think back. There was a time when *"no"* didn't bother you a bit. In fact, you relished receiving it because each *"no"* got you closer to the *"yes"* you wanted:

You (as a kid): *"Can I have a cookie, please?"*
Mom (acting parental): *"No, it will spoil your dinner."*

You (calling her bluff): *"It won't, I'll eat everything."*
Mom (she's heard that line before): *"No, it's too close to dinner time."*
You (determined to win): *"But I'm really hungry now!"*
Mom (weakening): *"One cookie, but you have to eat all of your vegetables."*
You (going for the kill): *"Even the beans? Ewww."*
Mom (caving): *"I'll give you a half portion of beans, but you must eat all of them."*
You (knowing a good deal): *"Okay."*
Mom (handing you the cookie): *"You'd better eat every one of those beans."*

In triumph, you take the cookie and go watch TV until dinner. Boy, you're good; you not only got that cookie, but you scored a bonus: tonight you only have to eat a half portion of those icky beans.

You got what you wanted and more because you refused to hear *"no."* You knew that if you were persistent enough, Mom would eventually give in and even if she didn't, you could always try again tomorrow.

But as you grew up, you not only began to hear *"no,"* you started to take it personally. And now when you get a *"no"* for reasons that have nothing to do with you, it's like a door has been slammed in your face, and all you want to do is go back to bed.

Reject Rejection

No doubt you've been rejected at least once in your life:

- You got stood up for a date.
- The person you're trying to date never calls you, returns your calls, emails you or responds to your emails.
- The person you are trying to have a relationship with won't see you, is never home and is dating someone else.

- The person you thought you had a relationship with moved without telling you that they moved, when they moved, where they moved to or how to reach them. Three weeks later, they call saying they've been "busy."

Rejection does not exist in business because rejection is personal, but business is all about transactions, usually involving money. What exists in business is a negative response that usually comes in the form of, "No, thank you."

If you are focusing the meeting on Mr. Bigg and he's doing the vast majority of the talking, any *"no"* you get most likely means, *"Not now,"* or *"I don't have enough information,"* or *"I don't have enough of the right information."* It never means, *"Go away; we hate you, you're a horrible person and don't ever contact anyone at this company for any reason ever again!"*

Despite your best efforts, you will probably get a few negative responses during your sales efforts. After all, not everyone needs your product or service right now or is smart enough to realize how great it would be to have it, and they're entitled to be wrong.

Chapter Fourteen
CLOSING IS JUST AN OPENING

Closing is the part of the sales process where you ask for the order. According to the Traditional System, the time to ask Mr. Bigg for a decision or feedback is after you've gone through your sales presentation and answered all of his objections.

The theory is that at this point, Mr. Bigg should be ready, willing and able to sign on the dotted line because he has no reason not to. But if he's still resistant, the Traditional System will have you maneuver Mr. Bigg into saying *"yes"* by using various kinds of closing tactics:[13]

> *Alternate Close: Offer the customer two choices, both of which are positive to the sale, rather than a yes or a no:*
> "Would you like the X or the Y model?"
> "Do you want to use your MasterCard or Visa?"
> "Would you like meet in the morning or the afternoon?"
> "Is Monday or Wednesday a better day for our next meeting?"
>
> *Assumptive Close: Begin to write up the sale without asking for the purchase. If they give their information, they are sold:*
> "What is your mailing address?"
> "What is your phone number with the area code first?
>
> *Minor/Major Close: This is very similar to a trial close; it merely ramps up the need:*
> "You can certainly agree that this is the best solution to your problem."

Challenge Close: Dares the customer to take action:
> "I understand that it's difficult to make a decision, I know that you're on the fence"
> "I know that it's difficult to change your life, however..."

Negative Close: Stress the disadvantage of failing to act. If the customer does nothing, their problems still exist, nothing changes and sometimes things may get worse. Show them the cost of not acting and not buying now:
> "The 20% discount will end tomorrow and it will cost you $xx more if you don't act now."

Emotional Close: Play on the customer's emotions:
> "You want to see your kids happy and smiling–don't you?"
> "If you get this, won't everyone just be so envious of you? You'll be the belle of the ball in that dress."

Ben Franklin Close: This is a comparison of the pluses and the minuses of something compared to each other. You list all the good (+) items on the left, then draw a line down the middle and list all the bad (-) items on the right side:
> "Let's look at the pluses and minuses on this, and then you decide."

You go through the pluses and then ask the customer to go through his minuses. Their list will be much smaller than yours and most likely, cost will be the focus. Absorb the cost into the money back guarantee and the other positives or break the cost down to its lowest common denominator and divide the cost by years, months, days, hours, minutes or even seconds. Use whichever one seems the most reasonable for the situation.

Worst Case/Best Case Scenario:
> Sales Rep: "What's the worst thing that could happen when you make this purchase?"

> *Prospect: "It doesn't work."*
> *Sales Rep: "Then you'd send it back for a refund."*
> *Prospect: "Right."*
> *Sales Rep: "And what's the best thing that could happen?"*
> *Prospect: "It works like you said."*
> *Sales Rep: "Exactly, did you want to go with the _____ or the _____?"*

A great salesperson will know all of these different closes, and at times will have to use several of them to get to the final close. Don't use the same one twice in a row. Mix it up. The only one that could be used several times in a row would be the alternate close when you are trying to narrow down a time for a meeting.

> *Sales Rep: "Would it be better to schedule our appointment on Monday or Thursday?"*
> *Prospect: "Let's make it on Thursday."*
> *Sales Rep: "Great, would morning or afternoon be better?"*
> *Prospect: "My afternoons are more open."*
> *Sales Rep: "Fine, then should we make it at 1:30 or at 3 o'clock?"*
> *Prospect: Will pick a time or make a different suggested time.*

Are You Being Sold?

Think back to a time when you bought something you really didn't want or need, but the salesperson was so good at closing that you bought it before you realized what was happening. Chances are that they used one or more of these closing techniques on you, and while they can be extremely effective, they're also extremely manipulative.

Since your goal is to develop a long lasting, mutually-beneficial relationship with Mr. Bigg from which sales flow naturally, you won't need to bother with the Traditional System's closing tactics. After all, if you don't like to be sold, neither does he.

Stop Selling and Let Him Buy

Whether or not Mr. Bigg buys what you're selling right then is irrelevant; what matters is the relationship you're forging with him. Mr. Bigg should feel so comfortable with you that even if he doesn't become your client now, he'll happily refer you to other people who will and may, in fact, come back to you at a later time.

This is why the buying decision should come from within Mr. Bigg, not be externally forced by you, and the decision to buy has to be on his timeframe, not yours.

"Now" is a matter of perspective in selling because there are simply too many factors outside your control that dictate when – or if – Mr. Bigg will be ready to move ahead.

In the Contrarian System, there is no need to maneuver Mr. Bigg into a *"yes"* because by the time you get to this point, he's already brought himself there.

Most of the time, when he does the talking and you do the listening, you've established a personal bond with him and laid the groundwork for doing business together.

This is why closing in the Contrarian System – assuming Mr. Bigg hasn't already talked himself into buying – is simply a matter of asking, *"Well, what do you think?"* and then waiting for the answer. Mr. Bigg will now give you what you've asked for – his honest feedback.

As you listen, he will bring up any issues, concerns, problems or resistance he didn't share with you before, tell you when to get back to him and/or explore with you how you two can make the deal happen.

---

*Far from being a "make it or break it" part of the sales process, closing should happen seamlessly. If you allow Mr. Bigg to buy instead of trying to sell him, getting the **"yes"** simply becomes a natural part of your on-going relationship with him.*

Part 4:
STAYING IN TOUCH

Chapter Fifteen
AFTER THE SALE

So you've made the sale, closed the deal and delivered the goods or provided the service. What happens now? Typically nothing, because in the Traditional System of selling, once a deal is done, you're on to the next sale. Essentially, you're virtually always starting from scratch.

Since it's the next sale that keeps you in business, you want to maximize the value of the sale you just made by planting the seeds for referrals and repeat business. Right after the sale, you and your client are in a sort of "honeymoon" phase – you're both feeling good about each other and want those warmies to continue as long as possible.

You can use many of the same tactics to generate referrals and repeat business as you did to generate leads. After all, your goal is to deepen and enrich your relationship with Mr. Bigg so he will spread that precious word of mouth about you and your business.

The most obvious follow-up would be right after you've made a sale, especially of products:

- Ensuring delivery of the product
- Checking on the performance of the product
- Training the customer how to use the product
- Making adjustments of mistakes in delivery quantity or quality
- Assisting with replacement parts and/or suggesting accessories or add-ons
- Helping to arrange and check displays (for sales to stores)
- Answering questions related to the product or other products or services your company provides

For service firms, following-up after the sale requires a little more creativity.

Send a Small Gift

Just like the painter who leaves a house plant after each finished job, find something that accentuates and enhances the experience your client has while using your product or service:

- A chiropractor doing an evaluation of a potential patient could provide free samples of nutritional supplements
- A hairdresser could give product samples provided by her suppliers
- A florist could give or email a guide to how to dry flowers
- A car dealer could send a coupon for two free oil changes at the dealership
- A Realtor could send a "How to Care for Your Home" guide with a maintenance checklist and a list of suggested local contractors, suppliers and do-it-yourself resources
- A family law attorney might send a book on handling the emotional side of divorce

Forward Relevant Information

If you're keeping up to date with what's happening in your area, be sure to let your past, present and future clients know what might affect them, such as major new projects, road construction and/or companies coming into town, plants shutting down or legislation that's been passed.

If your local Chamber of Commerce is putting on a seminar or special event that may interest your clients, let them know about it. Many local businesses would love to participate in festivals, carnivals and educational forums, but don't simply because they don't know about it or no one's asked them to attend or be involved.

Request Feedback

Shortly after the sale, think about emailing your client a survey form asking for their feedback. Many major retailers know that excellent customer service is the key to their ongoing success, so their online feedback forms focus on the experience of shopping at their stores, rather than the products they sell.

The same is true of many utilities which send you an email requesting feedback on the courteousness, knowledgeability and ability to serve you shortly after a conversation or online chat you've had with a customer service rep.

But while they are a handy tool, surveys tend to create an emotional distance between you and Mr. Bigg. He should feel comfortable enough to tell you directly what he thinks about the experience of buying from or working with you.

Stay in Touch

It's a good idea to call Mr. Bigg a week or two after the sale and ask him if he's happy with his purchase and/or the service you provided and if he has any questions. But don't stop there.

Since out of sight is out of mind, make it your responsibility to check in with Mr. Bigg by phone every six months or annually, especially if you sell a product that requires service, such as air conditioning/heating, water heaters, computers or cars, each of which require regularly scheduled maintenance to operate.

Spread the Word

Let other people know about your work in a way that's relevant to your business: if you're a contractor, put a sign in the yards of homes or buildings where you've done work, issue press releases and/or announce your accomplishment at your networking meetings, and so on.

Ask for Testimonials and Referrals

Testimonials are gold, so don't hesitate to ask for them. Most people don't know what to write, so suggest they comment on why they used your business, what problems it helped them to solve, the level of service they received and/or how they feel about buying from/working with you. Once you get testimonials, be sure to put them on your website and on your LinkedIn profile and/or Facebook page.

Since the post-sale honeymoon phase is the best time to ask for referrals, go on and ask, *"Who do you know who might want/benefit from/need _____?"* Chances are they know at least one other person, so be sure to have them write down their referrals for you.

Give Referrals

Make it a point to pass along referrals to your current, past and future clients whenever you can, and refer your colleagues in the industry if they can serve a client's needs better than you can. It will cost you nothing, and the good feeling you generate will be priceless. Eventually, you'll be known as an expert who generously spreads the wealth (in the form of referrals) around and as a source and as a resource of information.

Remember, what goes around comes around, so give your advice, knowledge, insights and referrals to whoever asks for it without expecting anything in return. You will be paid back a hundredfold in ways you can't even imagine.

Chapter Sixteen
THANK YOU VERY MUCH

Expressing your gratitude for a new client or customer is not just good manners; it makes great business sense. In situations where a purchase is made primarily on emotion, like apartment leasing services and senior living facilities, the company will send you a hand-written note thanking you simply for touring their property.

But often, a thank you note is nothing more than an expression of thanks when it has the potential to be so much more. Here are some sample Traditional System thank you notes for various sales situations:[14]

- *After setting an appointment over the phone: "Thank you for taking the time to talk with me on the phone yesterday, busy as you are. I look forward to our meeting next Tuesday at 10AM and promise to take only 15 minutes of your time."*

- *After an appointment when the prospect didn't buy: "Thank you for giving me the opportunity to tell you about my company's product. When you need a new [insert product here], I hope you will keep me in mind so that I will have the chance to provide you with excellent service."*

- *After an appointment when the prospect did buy: "Thank you for giving me the opportunity to offer you one of my company's exceptional products. I am certain you will benefit from our new relationship. If you have any questions about your [insert product here], please contact me immediately so that I can provide you with excellent service."*

- *After someone gives you a referral:* "Thank you for referring [insert referral name here] to me yesterday. You can be sure I will provide him/her with the highest quality of service possible."

- *After a prospect gives you a final "no":* "Thank you for taking the time to consider my company's product. I regret that we were not able to meet your current needs. Please feel free to call me if your situation changes or if you have any questions. I will keep in touch with any updates, as I hope that we will be able to do business together in the future."

- *After an existing customer buys again:* "Thank you for giving me the opportunity to once again serve you. I trust that we have continued to meet our own standards for exceptional service. Should you have any questions about your [insert product here], please contact me immediately so that I can assist you."

Rethink "Thank You"

A Traditional System thank you note is like a Traditional System sales letter–it's all about the person who is writing it, not the person who is reading it. But these notes contain something far more dangerous to your sales efforts–their tone implies you believe you are at the mercy of Mr. Bigg's whim and are helpless and powerless when it comes to making sales.

You should always express gratitude when someone does you a favor, gives you a gift or gives of themselves to you in some way. But Mr. Bigg did not do you a favor by buying or considering buying your product or service; he was simply conducting business.

Group Thank You's

What do you do if you've met with several Mr. Biggs at the same time, such as when you're selling to large companies or to a panel? The Traditional System tells you to send a different thank you note to each person or send one thank-you note to a key person for distribution to the others.

Well, the Traditional System has it half right. Group meetings can be intimidating, simply because you're having a conversation with several people at the same time, so there's very little opportunity to form a connection with any one of them.

Should you choose to contact members of the group after your meeting, you don't need to vary your letters to each one; just email the person who invited you to the meeting and copy the others, or email all of them together as a group. After all, that's how they met you.

If you meet with different people in different departments on a one-on-one basis, remember that they each have different perspectives on how your product or service can help them accomplish their goals. As a result, you will be writing something different to each person.

This should not be difficult if you treated each one as an individual Mr. Bigg and took notes as they talked. All you have to do now is feed back to them just what they told you and they'll think you're brilliant because you're thinking just like they do.

Chapter Seventeen
FOLLOW-UP LETTERS

In business, proposals are used when one company wants to hire another. A typical proposal includes:

- A summary of the client's situation as he told it to you
- A strategy for addressing the situation describing how your solutions or suggestions will be developed and delivered
- Biographies of the people doing the work and/or executives of your company
- A quote or estimate of the costs involved
- A timeline for completing the work
- References and/or other supporting material

Your follow-up letter should be the first part of a proposal in which you feed back to Mr. Bigg his description of his situation exactly as he told it to you without analysis, suggestions or solutions. This is why all those notes you took in the meeting are so important.

Writing Your Follow-Up Letter

The structure of a Contrarian System follow-up letter is very similar to that of a Contrarian System sales letter:

The Grabber: The first paragraph should be written to capture Mr. Bigg's attention and make him want to keep reading.

Recap Mr. Bigg's situation: Summarize Mr. Bigg's situation exactly as he described it to you without commenting on it.

Suggest your solution: Since you've already discussed with Mr. Bigg his problem or opportunity and how you might help him achieve his goals, you're simply reminding him of the benefits he told you he wants to have.

Assume the sale: You can remove any shred of doubt Mr. Bigg may still have by asserting that the two of you have a deal, even if nothing has been signed yet. The more confident you are about moving forward, the more Mr. Bigg will know he's made the right choice about working with you.

Here is a breakdown of a Contrarian System follow-up letter:

Contrarian System Follow Up Letter

The Grabber: "It was a real pleasure meeting with you yesterday. Given the many projects you are involved with, I really appreciate your fitting me into your tight schedule.

Recap Mr. Bigg's situation: "In our meeting, you described how Smith Products is experiencing challenges in merging the many accounting systems used by the small firms you have acquired over the last few years into one universal system.

"And of course, it's not just the technical issues involved here; the key to your on-going success will lie in ensuring that your employees embrace these changes through continuous training and motivation.

Suggest your solution: "As I explained, our ACE Accounting Software is designed to seamlessly integrate with your current systems, allowing your staff to perform at peak levels with minimal downtime for training.

Assume the Sale: "John, I appreciate your specific concerns as you remain competitive, and I look forward to working with you and your associates in helping Smith Products assert its rightful position as the country's top specialty producer of packaged goods."

"I versus You" score: I: 7, You: 17

Nailing the Deal

You may think you're being presumptuous by assuming that Mr. Bigg will buy your product or service. Not so. You're merely sharing your confidence that what you have is, in fact, what Mr. Bigg needs and that Mr. Bigg knows it.

On the other hand, if you're the slightest bit scared, worried or desperate, regardless of the words you use, Mr. Bigg will intuitively sense it and automatically doubt if your product or service is the solution to his problem. And you can be sure that doubt is the biggest deal killer there is.

But confidence is contagious, and when you truly believe that by working with you Mr. Bigg's problem is already solved, so will he.

Part 5:
ADDENDUM

Sales Secrets You Didn't Learn in Business School

By Janet White
President, The JW Speakers Agency
www.jwspeakersagency.com

Everybody is approachable with sincere flattery. There are no exceptions.

If you want to connect with someone you've never talked to before and start some sort of a business relationship with them, first learn about what's important to them and find something you can genuinely compliment them on. They'll love it.

If you want something, you must ask for it. The worst that can happen is that someone says, 'no,' but if they do, you will live.

The only person you should deal with is the one who has the authority to say "yes." Everyone else you will encounter has the ability to say "no," but they have no authority to say "yes." This is why you should always start at the top, and work down.

Truly important people have no egos, don't play power games and are easy to approach if you have something that will benefit them, their family or company and/or make them feel good. Best of all, they won't waste your time or theirs and will give you a clear, definitive answer.

Contrary to popular belief that you should expect a *"no"* in selling, the truth is that most people want to say *"yes"* because it makes them feel good.

It is very hard to say 'no" when being asked to do something that may benefit them, their family or their company and/or make them feel good.

No matter how important you think somebody is, to them, they are just another human being. If you've put someone on a pedestal, you're the one making them difficult to approach.

Powerful intermediaries who shield important people from the rest of the world are usually a figment of your imagination or turn out to be people who are just doing their job.

If there is a "gatekeeper," ask her name the first time you call and use it every time you call–she'll put you through with no problem or let you know why not.

If you want to achieve your goals, you must break out of your comfort zone. Your comfort zone is there to keep you safe, but it also keeps you small. We have a saying in our society to "think outside the box."

The truth is there is no box, except the one you decide you're in. You decide your limitations and you decide what's possible for you. The problem arises when you allow somebody else or society at large to determine the limits of your box.

When other people tell you, write, imply or suggest–with the best of intentions, mind you–that you shouldn't, you mustn't, you're not good enough, you'll never make it, you'll fail if you try and you'll be disappointed when you fail, remember that they are *not* talking about you; they're talking about themselves.

They're expressing their own fears, doubts and insecurities about what they believe is possible for them in that situation and are projecting their thoughts on you. You can't stop these people from sharing their negative thoughts, but you can stop yourself from allowing their opinions to become your beliefs. The best course of action is to listen to their "advice," and then ignore it.

These are the very same people who become absolutely astonished when you accomplish seemingly effortlessly what they considered to be impossible. And they would be right – it would have been impossible for them to what you did because they didn't believe they could.

Rejection does not exist in business because rejection is personal and business is all about transactions, usually involving money. Despite your best efforts, you will probably get a few negative responses in your sales efforts. Oh, well, life goes on and there's more opportunity just around the corner.

The secret to successful selling is to always remember:

In business as in life, the Golden Rule rules: treat everybody the way you want to be treated.

Nobody likes to be sold, but everybody loves to buy.

When you help someone get what they want, they will automatically and gratefully help you get what you want.

Traditional vs. Contrarian
SYSTEMS OF SELLING

The Traditional System	The Contrarian System
Cold calling is full of rejection	Cold calling is full of potential
Buyer is assumed to be at *"no"*	Buyer is assumed to be at *"yes"*
Seller is responsible for convincing buyer	Buyer convinces himself to buy
Seller makes a sales presentation about the product and how it can help the buyer	Seller has a conversation with buyer about the buyer's needs, interests and concerns
Approach is *"What we can do for you"*	Approach is *"How can we help you?"*
Focus is on the transaction	Focus is on the relationship
Buyer's human needs are ignored	Buyer's human needs are a major factor
Buyer resists cost of buying	Buyer appreciates the value of owning
Seller does most of the talking	Buyer does most of the talking
Seller uses pitching and pushiness	Seller uses persuasion and persistence
Seller wants the deal done ASAP	Buyer and seller determine the timing

The Traditional System	The Contrarian System
Seller believes that a lost sale is gone for good	Seller knows that no sale is ever lost because the buyer still has the need. Even if the buyer buys from someone else, the seller still has a good relationship with the buyer.
"No" means *"Go away"*	*"No"* means *"Not now"*
A lost sale is the seller's present failure	A lost sale is the seller's future opportunity

End Notes

1   Lynea Corson, George Hadley, Carl Stevens, *The Secrets of Super Selling* (Berkley Books, New York, 1991)
2   "SWOT Analysis Tips and Examples for Your Small Business" by Nicole Fallon, www.businessnewsdaily.com
3   "A Guide to Email Clients" by Monique Martin, www.hostway.com/web-resources/email-accounts/a-guide-to-email-clients
4   "8 Tips for Productive Sales Calls" by Wendy Connick, www.About.com/Sales
5   "12-Step Foolproof Sales Letter Template" by David Frey, www.marketingprofs.com/2/frey2.asp
6   "Part 1: Making the Perfect Follow-Up Call to Prospects" by Jim Domanski, http://www.fordyceletter.com/2012/04/11/part-1-making-the-perfect-follow-up-call-to-prospects
7   William "Skip" Miller, Ron Zemke, *Knock Your Socks Off Prospecting: How to Cold Call, Get Qualified Leads, and Make More Money* (*Knock Your Socks Off Service!*) (AMACOM 2005)
8   "How to Structure a Meeting for a Sales Presentation" by Sam Ashe-Edmunds, Demand Media http://work.chron.com/structure-meeting-sales-presentation-5136.html
9   "Dump The Script during Panel Presentations" by Tim Rohrer, www.salesgravy.com/sales-articles/presentation-skills/dump-the-script-during-panel-presentations.html
10 "How to Handle Objections in Six Easy Steps" by Wendy Connick, http://sales.about.com/od/salesbasics/ht/How-To-Handle-Objections-In-Six-Easy-Steps.htm
11 "Types of Sales Closes," http://gr8salestips.wordpress.com/2010/09/09/types-of-sales-closes
12 "Afraid of Rejection? Get Over It!" by Liz Wendling, www.salesgravy.com/sales-articles/women-only/afraid-of-rejection-get-over-it.html

13 "Types of Sales Closes," http://gr8salestips.wordpress.com/2010/09/09/types-of-sales-closes

14 "Sample Thank-You Notes by Wendy Connick, http://sales.about.com/od/salesbasics/a/Sample-Thank-You-Notes.htm

www.ingramcontent.com/pod-product-compliance
Lightning Source LLC
Chambersburg PA
CBHW071710090426
42738CB00009B/1731